JESUS IS LORD

THE CRY OF A KINGDOM CITIZEN

FRANK MOORE WITH BRENT MOORE

BEACON HILL PRESS
OF KANSAS CITY

Cover Design: Ryan Deo
Interior Design: Sharon Page

This book is dedicated to our grandchildren.
"So each generation should set its hope anew on God"
(Ps. 78:7a, NLT).
May Mia and Micah come to know what Marley knows so well—
Jesus is Lord!

*But watch out! Be careful never to forget what you yourself have seen.
Do not let these memories escape from your mind as long as you live!
And be sure to pass them on to your children and grandchildren.*
—Deut. 4:9, NLT

CONTENTS

FOREWORD

When the fabric of the church is stretched and tested by the winds of convulsing change, some things remain uncontested, unchanged, and uncompromised. The lordship of Jesus Christ remains the continuing constant that preserves the church, Christ's body, from the effects of those forces that would compromise its integrity.

Frank Moore writes with power, understanding, and passion. From deep within his intellect, as well as his heart, comes this ringing testimony to the lordship of Christ. Dr. Moore explores the full range of our Lord's royal authority that translates into fresh insights and subtle reminders of the church's allegiance to its King.

Every Christian will benefit from the study of this topic. The abrasive power of an alien culture threatens the church in every age. When believers are armed both with the power of the Spirit and the presence of the Word, the church does more than just retain its spiritual soundness. Under Christ's banner, the church perseveres and will fulfill its earthly mission.

—Dr. David Graves
General Superintendent
Church of the Nazarene

PREFACE

I completed my research and began writing this book several years ago. One morning, in the middle of my writing session, the telephone rang. Our son, Brent, called to give us bad news about our eighteen-month-old granddaughter, Marley. While having a routine well-baby visit at the doctor's office, something abnormal surfaced. Brent and Nikki, his wife, immediately took Marley to the children's hospital. The first test revealed a malignant brain tumor.

Sue and I dropped everything and quickly drove to Kansas City to support our kids. This book went into a box under my desk for three years. Our journey with Marley during that time was filled with both high and low times emotionally. We learned to cherish every minute of every day with her. She taught us a lifetime of lessons about the meaning of life and faith in Christ. We each grew in remarkable ways from that blessed but difficult journey we walked together.

A few weeks after we returned from the cemetery, I got the box of random thoughts of this book out from under my desk. I decided it was time to write again. I realized as I started writing that Marley cast her impression on every page. You see, the lordship of Christ has taken on an entirely different meaning for me as a result of Marley's life. Now I think of Jesus not only as Lord over all the areas you are going to read about in this book but also as the One who presently has the care of my precious granddaughter.

Marley reminds me daily to keep heaven's values in mind, to not hold too tightly to this world's goods, and to long for the things important to God. All of these reminders point me to the lordship of

Christ on a daily basis. That is why I say Marley impacted everything I wrote. That is why I asked Brent to write the last chapter. I wanted you to hear a dad's perspective on this subject. How does our family say "Jesus is Lord" after what we have experienced? I know many readers have experienced similar or related losses in life. I trust you will be encouraged and offered a word of hope as you read Brent's words.

I continue to be in debt to my wonderful wife, Sue, who supports me completely in my writing ministry. She brainstorms concepts with me, clears my calendar to write, and proofs with the eye of an eagle. I could never write without her undying love and support. Ours is a team ministry. Our whole family prays that you will be blessed and changed by this book and that somehow through it Marley will impact you as much as she impacted us.

—Frank Moore

In your relationships with one another, have the same mindset as
Christ Jesus:
  Who, being in very nature God,
      did not consider equality with God something to be used to
          his own advantage;
  rather, he made himself nothing
      by taking the very nature of a servant,
      being made in human likeness.
  And being found in appearance as a man,
      he humbled himself
      by becoming obedient to death—
          even death on a cross!
  Therefore God exalted him to the highest place
      and gave him the name that is above every name,
  that at the name of Jesus every knee should bow,
      in heaven and on earth and under the earth,
  and every tongue acknowledge that Jesus Christ is Lord,
      to the glory of God the Father.
                              —Phil. 2:5-11

SO MANY LORDS

So God created mankind in his own image, in the image of God he created them; male and female he created them.
—Gen. 1:27

The twenty-first century is now well underway, and Christians are everywhere. They have spread throughout the world and are found on every continent, speaking nearly every language known to humanity. Two thousand or so years have passed since Jesus walked along the shores of Galilee, and during that time his message has taken root in countless hearts. Starting with eleven disciples—twelve minus the one who betrayed him—Jesus grew his church to where it is today. He filled his disciples and those who followed after them with the Holy Spirit. Empowered by that Spirit, ordinary Christians—like you and me—down through the centuries have reached others with the good news about Jesus. Ours is an incredible heritage!

Perhaps the most common phrase that has united all of us everywhere and in every time is "Jesus is Lord." That phrase appears in more languages and more countries than any other. From large sanctuaries filled with suburban believers to thatched-roof churches packed with rural worshippers, the message remains the same around the world: Jesus is Lord!

Lost in Translation

But now that we've moved into the twenty-first century, something has changed. It's been a quiet and a subtle change. But the change has been no less dramatic. Our contemporary culture has somehow lost its capacity to adequately interpret the word "lord" for us. We just don't know what it really means anymore. Something has been lost in translation. No word in our modern languages carries all of the rich meaning of the words found in biblical language. So we need to take a new look and explore the concept and its meaning for us today.

It's easy to conform to our Christian heritage and say, "Jesus is Lord." It's not as easy, however, to put those words into daily action. What do we mean when we say that Jesus is Lord of everything in our world? And how do we make him Lord of our daily words and deeds? That's what we're going to explore in the pages ahead. We need to understand today, just as much as Jesus' first disciples did, what it means to apply this confession of faith to our everyday lives.

Timeless

Some things in contemporary culture change, but other things don't. Human nature, for instance, remains timelessly the same. People next door act about the way people did in Abraham's day—four thousand years ago. Relationships are another thing that doesn't change. Human beings get together to talk, laugh, cry, and just be in one another's presence. We like to play together, shop together, and eat together. And when we can't be with one another, we send greeting cards, presents, and letters. We also send emails, make phone calls, or use video calling. But best of all, when we can't be together in person, we like to connect through Facebook. Millions of us from around the world use Facebook to keep up with one another, renew old acquaintances, and make new friends.

All of us have quiet and reflective moments from time to time. Maybe the death of a loved one causes us to stop and reflect on life. Or maybe something good happens that causes us to stop and count our blessings. Whatever the occasion may be, we usually realize that the most important realities in our lives are the relationships we have with the people we know and love. These relationships soar in value far above any job titles, awards, possessions, or educational degrees. Why? Because God made us as relational beings. He made us in his image, as Gen. 1:27 tells us. Father, Son, and Spirit relate to one another in an intimate way. We, too, are hardwired for relationships with one another. That being said, we experience an eerie feeling that something is not right with life when human relationships are missing from our lives.

A certain insurance actuary, for example, sits in his office cubical all day and crunches numbers to predict the probable life expectancies of others. Although this man has everything in life that money can buy, he's not happy. His life is missing relationships. "Without relationships," he says, "I have nothing." Even though people may urge him to go out and enjoy spending his big paycheck, he knows better. Life's true meaning is not found in money or the things it can purchase; we find life's meaning through relationships.

University students going on mission trips to underdeveloped countries often gain a new perspective about the importance of relationships.[1] They go to build churches and schools and do compassionate ministries. They work manually alongside the local people, interacting with them and playing and worshipping together. Students often wonder, at the start of such trips, how the people they are going to work with can be so happy with so few material possessions, but by the end of the trip the students usually realize that the people are very rich relationally: (1) they have a relationship with Jesus as Lord of their lives, (2) they have relationships with their family members, and (3) they have relationships with one another in the community of faith. As far as the people are concerned, they have everything they need. Why would they need material possessions to be happy? What do material possessions have to do with happiness, anyway?

As Christians we know the importance of relationships, both with our family members and with members of our community of faith. Our most important relationship, however, is with Jesus Christ. We must start with him.

Jesus First

Jesus makes possible a relationship with our heavenly Father. Once we have firmly established that relationship, we can sort out the broken pieces in our own hearts and heads so that we can become whole persons inwardly. Then we can relate properly to ourselves. Once we are on the road to wholeness within ourselves, we move outwardly to our family members and start to build strong relationships with them. From family members, we move on to friends and acquaintances in the world to build strong relationships with them. Never forget that all of those relationships flow, like spokes from a wheel, from our primary relationship with Jesus Christ. We must nurture our relationship with him first. Only then are we healthy enough to build relationships with others.

If Jesus serves as our primary relationship, then he must be Lord over all of our lives. He must be the lens through which we view all of life. He must be the One to whom we offer our primary and complete commitment. We say that in theory as we talk together in our small-group meetings. It's harder to put in daily practice. Why? Because we have to make so many quick choices each day—and we find so many lords competing for our allegiance.

So Many Lords

Life in contemporary culture keeps us preoccupied with so many daily activities. We have so many options, so many authorities, so many truths, and so many lords. We must keep our bearings as we negotiate the ever-shifting seas of our information and communication explosion. We have so much coming at us so quickly each day.

This issue of lordship is not just a matter affecting the culture of the United States and Canada, Western Europe, and other developed nations. It affects our entire world. More than ever before in human history, the nations and cultures of the world have become interdependent on one another. At one time, individual families lived much to themselves and supplied most of their own needs. They lived and died as self-contained family units. Their reliance on other people and outside resources was limited.[2]

That's seldom true anywhere in the world today. Watch the morning news. Global stock markets impact one another every hour of the business day. The daily price of crude oil makes the news on every television station in the world. Ecology issues, like climate change and resource management, affect nearly every culture of the world. Satellite television, cell phone technology, Internet connectivity, and economical air travel unite all the peoples of the earth in amazing ways.[3]

Perhaps that's part of the reason for the global shift that is shrinking our world. Maybe it's because of worldwide, seamless communication through the Internet and cell phones. Perhaps it's because of the dramatic increase in jet travel that takes us to faraway places in a few short hours. Perhaps it's because of great migrations of people around the world. No doubt, there are many factors, but what is clear is that we are the most connected people in human history. Our world is shrinking at lightning speed!

Added to this new reality is the increased attention and visibility the religions of the world are receiving. Once considered as belonging to somewhere faraway, in distant lands, now the religions of the world are as near as our neighborhood grocery stores. Their places of worship are in our cities, towns, and rural areas, and their worshippers can be found reading their sacred books and saying their prayers in almost any airport. In all of this religious diversity, who is Lord?

The Big Blue Globe

Think for a minute about this big, blue globe we call planet earth. Who is Lord of it? Who oversees its daily preservation? Do you think of that often? And who oversees the nations of the world? Are they left to manage the best way they can? Who is Lord over the global issues that most worry our scientists? Who is Lord over things that can so easily get out of hand, like technology or pandemic diseases? These and dozens of other big-picture questions remind us that we need a Lord big enough to care for these matters that are bigger than any and all of us.

We also live in an environment of competing value systems and worldviews. The business world has its lords. The television industry has its lords. The movie industry has its lords. So do the worlds of sports, advertising, and finance. The same is true for the worlds of education, music, and politics. The list is endless! Will we Christians pay our respect and give our time and money to these lords or will we save our allegiance for Another? That's a question that demands an answer.

From time to time scientists on television or in the newspaper predict the end of life on earth as we know it. Some speak of using up all of the energy stored in the earth. Others speak of running out of clean air to breathe or clean water to drink. Some say a giant meteor will smash into the earth. Others say the sun may burn out. Some say crazy people with the keys to atomic bombs will blow us all to kingdom come.

Whether or not any of these self-proclaimed authorities have their facts straight is uncertain. But what is certain is that each of us is going to come to the end of this life someday. And the evidence seems to indicate that life as we know it on this earth right now also has a termination day. What then? Who is Lord of the future? Furthermore, who is Lord of the next life?

Finding Answers

You're not going to get answers to any of these questions from the contemporary culture. It doesn't know. It asks many questions and questions many theories but offers few answers. It seems to be uncertain about pretty much everything. Those of us who call ourselves Christian need to think about our responses to these questions from a Christian perspective and offer biblical responses. We can know some things for sure when it comes to this matter of lordship.

In the pages ahead, we'll explore these and other topics. First, we'll turn our attention to examples of Christians declaring "Jesus is Lord" in their confessions, creeds, and statements of faith. Then we'll turn to the Bible for insights into the concept of lordship from both the Old and New Testaments. Next, we will explore the many domains over which Jesus exercises lordship. Finally, we will devote the rest of the book to a personal application of these thoughts to our lives and examine practical ways to make Jesus Lord over every aspect of daily living.

THINK ABOUT THIS

1. What qualities, desires, and interests about people do not change with time?

2. Why are relationships so important to human beings?

3. Why do people in developed nations often think material possessions are required for happiness in life?

4. How do you manage big-picture questions such as, Who is Lord of the daily preservation of planet earth?

5. Why does contemporary culture ask many questions but offer few answers?

PRACTICE THIS

1. For one entire day keep a log of how many choices you make. Write down the times of day, the options, and the selections you made. At the end of the day, total the number of choices you made that day. You will be amazed at the sheer number. Look over the list. Analyze it. How many were really important? How many involved much thought? How many brought stress? How many were of eternal value? How many had moral implications? How many had spiritual implications? More specifically, how many affected your commitment to making Jesus Lord of your life?

2. For one entire day keep a log of how many truth claims come your way. Remember the sources, such as news reports, advertisements, the Internet, Facebook, blogs, phone calls, and books. Examples of truth claims might include, "This car is safer," "This drink tastes better," and "This dress is cheaper." Write down the source and one word that will jog your memory for each truth claim. At the end of the day, total the number of truth claims you received that day. How many truth claims did you hear? How many did you really believe? How many were important to you? How many had moral implications?

How many had spiritual implications? How many affected your commitment to make Jesus Lord of your life?

PART ONE

A CHRISTIAN UNDERSTANDING OF LORDSHIP IN THE BIBLE AND CHRISTIAN TRADITION

Part One will look at the confession "Jesus is Lord" as it is used today and then trace the idea back to its origins in the early creeds of the Christian faith. We will take a look at the roots of our Christian heritage in the early days of the church. We will also study the concept of lordship as it is found in both the Old and New Testaments, paying particular attention to the way individual narratives illustrate the concept. We will further look at several areas over which Christ is Lord in our world in the interval between the "already" and the "not yet"; that is, between the inauguration of the kingdom of God in Christ and its future consummation. Since we live in the in-between time of these two periods, we can easily forget that Jesus is Lord both now and forever over these areas of life.

CHAPTER TWO

CREEDS, DOCTRINES, AND OTHER FAITH STUFF

If you declare with your mouth,

"Jesus is Lord," and believe

in your heart that God raised

him from the dead, you

will be saved.

—Rom. 10:9

A number of years ago, teens in church camps and group gatherings were introduced to a new arrangement of an old chorus. It was sung repeatedly, and its lyrics were stamped on the memories of scores of young people. To this day many of these people still remember the words, and others are learning and singing "He Is Lord" in Christian gatherings around the world. Possibly it is sung in more languages than any other chorus. But whether or not that is so, it still rings true in every language, in every land.

> He is Lord, He is Lord!
> He is risen from the dead and He is Lord!
> Ev'ry knee shall bow, ev'ry tongue confess
> That Jesus Christ is Lord.[1]

Nobody knows the actual origin of this chorus, but the declaration certainly has an ancient history. In fact, it stands as the oldest Christian confession of church history. From the very beginning of the church age, believers have been stepping forward to proclaim, "Jesus is Lord."

We have numerous references to this statement in the books of the New Testament. In chapter 4 of this book, we will take a detailed look at the confession in some of these Scripture passages. For now, suffice it to say that Christians at the time the books of the New Testament were being written laid claim to this powerful confession of faith.

Caesar Is Lord

Many believe the early church maintained the acclamation "Jesus is Lord" because of what was happening in the political world. At that time, leaders of the Roman Empire needed a way to unite its citizens around a common cause that would engender their allegiance. It's sort of like the owner of a professional sports team needing a way to encourage the combined allegiance of people to the team: "How about those Bears?" or "Go Cubs!"

Perhaps highly recommended marketing experts got together from around the empire and brainstormed strategies to unite the empire's many language and culture groups. The leaders or experts finally decided to unite the diverse populations with a common allegiance to the emperor, and they selected the phrase "Caesar is Lord" for the campaign slogan. It became a public chant everywhere—at local sporting events, political gatherings, and social functions. People greeted one another with it as they met in the marketplace or courtyard. You might think such a declaration could be interpreted as nothing more than a patriotic gesture. People often do this today when they sing their national anthem at public gatherings. They are acknowledging their loyalty to the government but nothing more.

The chant "Caesar is Lord" wasn't as generically patriotic as that, however. No, "Caesar is Lord" implied the total allegiance of its citizens—including the spiritual component of their lives. The chant had enough of a religious tone to it that early Christians found themselves in a tough spot. They couldn't make the declaration without compromising their allegiance to Christ. So they refused to fall into line as good citizens of the Roman Empire and declare their total commitment to the empire's chief ruler. Instead, they substituted their own chant, which proclaimed their ultimate allegiance: "Jesus is Lord."

As you might imagine, this was unacceptable to the Roman officials. They informed the Christians that they were falling short of their obligation to Rome and its authority. The Christians responded that they couldn't be divided in their loyalty. "We can't serve two lords," they said. They only had room in their hearts for one Lord, and his name was Jesus. Rome warned of serious sanctions if the Christians didn't submit and adopt the new slogan declaring their allegiance to Caesar.

The Christians held firm to their convictions. Many of them lost their jobs, many more lost their possessions, and some even lost their lives. You might say they sealed their allegiance with their blood. They just would not back down. And so today, when Christians make the declaration "Jesus is Lord," they are placing themselves in the long, rich heritage of those who paid a high price for their unswerving faithfulness.

The New Testament Credo

What was the background for the early Christian church's bold and life-altering confession that Jesus is Lord? Clearly, the New Testament Scriptures provided a wealth of information for building such a confession. Later, we will take a thorough look at scriptural insights into this truth, but for now we will concentrate on the simple statement itself.

The most basic of the New Testament confessions is found in Rom. 10:9: "If you declare with your mouth, 'Jesus is Lord,' and believe in your heart that God raised him from the dead, you will be saved." Notice that Paul connected Christ's lordship to his resurrection. Take special note of this; it is extremely important. Often we find long lists stating what Christians believe about Jesus Christ. We give these lists titles, such as Articles of Faith. Later in this chapter, we will look at some of the confessions of faith that list doctrines important for all Christians to believe.

Think for a minute. If someone asked you to select the most important of your Christian beliefs and place it at the top of a list, what would you say? That's what Paul is doing in this verse. The Christian belief at the top of Paul's list, after saying "Jesus is Lord," was God raised Jesus from the dead. This reminds us of the central role Christ's resurrection played in establishing the faith of the early church.

It is no coincidence that Christ's resurrection and the idea of believing in it occur together in this verse. German biblical scholar Hans Conzelmann calls verses like this "credo" because they refer to the saving acts of our Christian faith. The main features of this particular credo are (1) God is the subject, (2) "raised" is a once-and-for-all event in time, and (3) Christ was raised from death to new life.[2] Numerous passages throughout the New Testament offer similar creedal statements.[3]

Early Christians treated the credo statement "Jesus is Lord" as an acclamation, or statement of praise, of their belief that Jesus is divine and their Savior. This credo statement became their act of worship. Tradition even tells us that they bowed their knees as they proclaimed this statement of faith in Christ.[4]

This statement served a variety of purposes in the early church. In Phil. 2:6-11, we see the statement used as an act of worship. In Rom. 10:8-13, we see it used as sermon content. In 1 Cor. 12:3, it served as a test of a person's orthodox adherence to the Christian faith.[5]

Now let's examine a more complex statement as another example of the way the early church incorporated their Christian beliefs into their affirmation that Jesus is Lord.

First Corinthians 15:3-8 reads,

For what I received I passed on to you as of first importance: that Christ died for our sins according to the Scriptures, that he was buried, that he was raised on the third day according to the Scriptures, and that he appeared to Cephas, and then to the Twelve. After that, he appeared to more than five hundred of the brothers and sisters at the same time, most of whom are still living, though some have fallen asleep. Then he appeared to James, then to all the apostles, and last of all he appeared to me also, as to one abnormally born.

Within this more developed faith proclamation we see several observations: (1) Christ died, (2) he was buried, (3) he was raised, and (4) he appeared to many of his followers. All of these statements are part of a fuller understanding of what Christ did to bring about our salvation. Paul's letters offered several variations of these events. Though the combinations differed, Paul's purposes remained the same; that is, Paul wanted to affirm that Christ's incarnation purchased our salvation. And as a result, Christ's followers now proclaimed him as Lord.[6]

The Early Christian Church

Let's take a closer look at the statement "Jesus is Lord" and analyze it according to the way early Christians intended it as they witnessed to the world and submitted themselves to God in worship. Jesus is the person who holds the title and rank of Lord. Or looking at it from the perspective of logic, as a propositional statement, "Jesus" is the subject and "Lord" is the affirmation about him.

We see more taking place here than a simple statement of belief that the Father raised him from the dead, as we saw in Rom. 10:9. Rather, the early Christians used the statement as a direct invocation of acclaiming his majesty. By "acclaiming" we mean, they made the statement as an act of tribute and prostration before him in submission.[7] This analysis adds four important words to our discussion: "worship," "majesty," "tribute," and "submission."

We are using the word "acclaim" here because the original Greek words of the New Testament mean "to praise" or "to applaud" (Rom. 14:11; 15:9), "to acclaim" (Phil. 2:11), or "to make a firm agreement or deal" (Luke 22:6). When we looked at Rom. 10:9, the most basic confession of faith for the early church, Jesus is called Lord, not in relation to his saving work for us, but as an acclaim of faith by his followers. They wanted to bestow on him both status and significance.[8]

So now we have another use of the statement "Jesus is Lord" by early Christians. It served as an act of worship that speaks to their relationship with him and their desire to lift him to a place of honor in their worship services. Hence, the statement is both a confession of faith and a declaration of allegiance. It is both the preaching point of a sermon and a shout of praise. This allegiance made Christ Lord over all other lords in an exclusive way. This is why his followers gladly endured martyrdom for him.[9]

The Apostles' Creed

The Apostles' Creed is one of the earliest creeds of the Christian faith. It offers us a basic list of beliefs about Christianity that unites us as brothers and sisters at the foot of the cross. All Christians should know this simple creed.

It's not the earliest confession of Christianity. Perhaps the earliest creed-like statement came in answer to Jesus' question to Peter at Caesarea Philippi when he asked, "Who do people say the Son of Man is?" (Matt. 16:13). Simon Peter answered, "You are the Messiah, the Son of the living God" (v. 16). Peter's confession was similar to a creed because it was a public statement of his faith. It wasn't technically a creed, however. While creeds are public statements of our Christian faith, they are decided by large councils of the church and affirmed over time.

The Apostles' Creed cannot be traced back authoritatively to the time of the apostles. There are legendary stories of the apostles writing phrases of this creed on the tenth day after Christ's ascension into heaven. These stories, however, cannot be validated. The earliest written version of this creed was found in the Interrogatory Creed of Hippolytus, dating back to AD 215. The current form of the creed is found in the writing of Caesarius of Arles, who died in AD 542. We believe the creed came from baptismal catechisms. Hence, new believers would have memorized this creed before being baptized into the Christian faith. Here is a current translation of the Apostles' Creed:

> I believe in God, the Father almighty,
>> creator of heaven and earth.
> I believe in Jesus Christ, his only Son, our Lord.
>> He was conceived by the power of the Holy Spirit
>>> and born of the Virgin Mary.
>> He suffered under Pontius Pilate,
>>> was crucified, died, and was buried.
>> He descended to the dead.
>> On the third day he rose again.
>> He ascended into heaven,
>>> and is seated at the right hand of the Father.
>> He will come again to judge the living and the dead.
> I believe in the Holy Spirit,
>> the holy catholic Church,
>> the communion of saints,
>> the forgiveness of sins,

the resurrection of the body,
and the life everlasting. Amen.[10]

Notice the creed is Trinitarian. It is built on the three-part out-line of Father, Son, and Holy Spirit. Notice that as soon as the Son is introduced into the creed, he is named as the Father's Son and then as our Lord. The early Christians established Christ's lordship first and foremost in his identity. Before they tell of

his incarnation on our earth,

his passion before Pontius Pilate,

his atonement on the cross,

his resurrection,

his ascension to heaven,

his reunion with the Father, or

the coming judgment,

they establish his lordship. Yes, to the early Christians Christ's lord-ship shaped everything they believed about Jesus. Thus his lordship permeated this early creed.

The Nicene Creed

About three hundred years after Jesus returned to his Father in heaven, Christians assembled for their first ecumenical council. Later known as the First Council of Nicaea, this gathering of the church in AD 325 was for the purpose of crafting a creed of the faith. Much had happened in the world and in the church. The Christian faith had spread in amazing ways. It also had encountered increased opposition in the form of persecution and false teachers; opponents had tried to twist Christian beliefs into heresy and dethrone Jesus as Lord. They offered other lords in his place.

Christian officials worked for many years to get the language of this creed just right in order to counter the opposition. In AD 381, they gathered again at the First Council of Constantinople and add-ed several words that shaped the creed into what we know today as the Nicene Creed. Here is a recent translation.

We believe in one God,
    the Father, the Almighty,
    maker of heaven and earth,
    of all that is, seen and unseen.
We believe in one Lord, Jesus Christ,
    the only Son of God,
    eternally begotten of the Father,
    God from God, Light from Light,
    true God from true God,
    begotten, not made,
    of one Being with the Father.
    Through him all things were made.
    For us and for our salvation
        he came down from heaven:
    by the power of the Holy Spirit
        he became incarnate from the Virgin Mary,
        and was made man.
For our sake he was crucified under Pontius Pilate;
    he suffered death and was buried.
    On the third day he rose again
        in accordance with the Scriptures;
    he ascended into heaven
        and is seated at the right hand of the Father.
    He will come again in glory to judge the living and the dead,
        and his kingdom will have no end.
We believe in the Holy Spirit, the Lord, the giver of life,
    who proceeds from the Father and the Son.
    With the Father and the Son he is worshiped and glorified.
    He has spoken through the Prophets.
    We believe in one holy catholic and apostolic Church.
    We acknowledge one baptism for the forgiveness of sins.
    We look for the resurrection of the dead,
        and the life of the world to come. Amen.[11]

You notice right away that when comparing the Apostles' Creed with the Nicene Creed, the later one has much more detail. This reminds us of the heresies that arose in the early days of the church to call true doctrine into question. This first ecumenical creed attempted to reaffirm true doctrine by adding definitive words in key places.

Look at the first mention of Jesus Christ. The creed begins by calling him Lord! This creed established that first and foremost. It declared many things about him that affirmed his honored status:

- He is the only begotten Son of God.
- He was begotten before God created the worlds.
- He was not made, as created things are, but begotten.
- He and the Father have the same substance.

The rest of the section about Jesus reads much like the Apostles' Creed. However, once you begin reading the section about the Holy Spirit, you notice something very different from the Apostles' Creed. That is, the section on the Spirit calls attention to the fact that the Holy Spirit proceeds from the Father and the Son. This references Christ's honored divine status. The creed further calls attention to the fact that the Son is worshipped and glorified together with the Father and the Spirit. No one can doubt that the early Christian church worshipped Jesus as Lord at the time the Councils of Nicaea and Constantinople met.

The Athanasian Creed

This third creed from the early church is included along with the other two to provide a clear picture of just how highly the church regarded the lordship of Jesus Christ. We do not know the date of this creed for sure. As you can see, it has much more detail than the other creeds. It countered all of the controversy and heresy offered against Jesus at that time. It also presented a clear doctrine of Christ. That is why it is so important. Notice how highly it exalted Christ and called on us to worship him as the one true God.

This creed affirmed everything the other creeds stated, so we need not comment again on what was stated earlier. Read through the creed. Several observations are included at the end on some words and concepts that this creed employed to remind us that Jesus is Lord. This creed is much longer than the previous two due to the extreme opposition it was mustering against false teachers trying to undermine the exclusive lordship of Christ. As you read, keep in mind that other lords were being offered for worship in that day.

> Whosoever will be saved, before all things it is necessary that he hold the Catholic Faith.
>
> Which Faith except everyone do keep whole and undefiled, without doubt he shall perish everlastingly.
>
> And the Catholic Faith is this: That we worship one God in Trinity, and Trinity in Unity, neither confounding the Persons, nor dividing the Substance.
>
> For there is one Person of the Father, another of the Son, and another of the Holy Ghost.
>
> But the Godhead of the Father, of the Son, and of the Holy Ghost is all one, the Glory equal, the Majesty coeternal.
>
> Such as the Father is, such is the Son, and such is the Holy Ghost.
>
> The Father uncreated, the Son uncreated, and the Holy Ghost uncreated.
>
> The Father incomprehensible, the Son incomprehensible, and the Holy Ghost incomprehensible.
>
> The Father eternal, the Son eternal, and the Holy Ghost eternal.
>
> And yet they are not three eternals, but one eternal.
>
> As also there are not three incomprehensibles, nor three uncreated, but one uncreated, and one incomprehensible.
>
> So likewise the Father is Almighty, the Son Almighty, and the Holy Ghost Almighty.
>
> And yet they are not three Almighties, but one Almighty.
>
> So the Father is God, the Son is God, and the Holy Ghost is God.
>
> And yet they are not three Gods, but one God.
>
> So likewise the Father is Lord, the Son Lord, and the Holy Ghost Lord.
>
> And yet not three Lords, but one Lord.
>
> For like as we are compelled by the Christian verity to acknowledge every Person by himself to be both God and Lord,
>
> So are we forbidden by the Catholic Religion, to say, There are three Gods, or three Lords.
>
> The Father is made of none, neither created, nor begotten.
>
> The Son is of the Father alone, not made, nor created, but begotten.
>
> The Holy Ghost is of the Father and of the Son, neither made, nor created, nor begotten, but proceeding.

So there is one Father, not three Fathers; one Son, not three Sons; one Holy Ghost, not three Holy Ghosts.

And in this Trinity none is afore, or after another; none is greater, or less than another;

But the whole three Persons are coeternal together and coequal.

So that in all things, as is aforesaid, the Unity in Trinity and the Trinity in Unity is to be worshipped.

He therefore that will be saved must thus think of the Trinity.

Furthermore it is necessary to everlasting salvation that he also believe rightly the Incarnation of our Lord Jesus Christ.

For the right Faith is, that we believe and confess, that our Lord Jesus Christ, the Son of God, is God and Man;

God, of the Substance of the Father, begotten before the worlds; and Man, of the Substance of his Mother, born in the world,

Perfect God, and perfect Man, of a reasonable soul and human flesh subsisting;

Equal to the Father, as touching his Godhead; and inferior to the Father, as touching his Manhood.

Who although he be God and Man, yet he is not two, but one Christ;

One, not by conversion of the Godhead into flesh, but by taking of the Manhood into God;

One altogether; not by confusion of Substance, but by unity of Person.

For as the reasonable soul and flesh is one man, so God and Man is one Christ;

Who suffered for our salvation, descended into hell, rose again the third day from the dead.

He ascended into heaven, he sitteth on the right hand of the Father, God Almighty, from whence he will come to judge the quick and the dead.

At whose coming all men shall rise again with their bodies and shall give account for their own works.

And they that have done good shall go into life everlasting; and they that have done evil into everlasting fire.

This is the Catholic Faith, which except a man believe faithfully, he cannot be saved.[12]

The Athanasian Creed affirmed without question the exclusive lordship of Christ! He is the second member of the Trinity and thus deserves our worship. He shares heavenly glory with the Father and the Spirit. He shares the coeternal majesty with the Father and the Spirit. He is incomprehensible. That doesn't mean we can't know anything about Jesus; it means we can't know everything about him. We will never master him with our understanding.

He is eternal, both before and after the created order. During his incarnation on this earth, he was perfect God and perfect man. Now that he has ascended back to his Father, he is almighty. He is God. He is Lord! No one can doubt that this early confession of faith recognized Jesus as equal to God in every way.

Conclusion

In this chapter we have examined the early days of the church, beginning with the New Testament. We reviewed the church at work hammering out the language of its faith across several hundred years of early Christian tradition. These were difficult days for Christians as they struggled against persecutions, oppositions, and false teachers. The Holy Spirit remained faithful to them and brought them through all of the opposition, with their faith intact and their doctrine sound. We have the creeds of the early Christian church as a reminder of their faithfulness to Christ.

Some critics have argued that modern Christians have tried to enhance Jesus' image to improve his status among world religions and that they are doing this to gain converts to Christianity. Nothing could be further from the truth. Christians from the earliest days of Christianity have affirmed that Jesus is Lord of all. Christians today are just following in that long tradition.

Today we continue the tradition and pass it on to our children. We will teach them the creeds of the Christian faith and the choruses that proclaim,

> *He is Lord, He is Lord!*
> *He is risen from the dead and He is Lord!*
> *Ev'ry knee shall bow, ev'ry tongue confess*
> *That Jesus Christ is Lord.*[13]

THINK ABOUT THIS

1. If you have sung the chorus "He Is Lord," what are your first memories of learning it?

2. What is the significance of that chorus to you?

3. Go back in time in your mind. If required by the government, would you have publically declared, "Caesar is Lord"? Why? Why not?

4. Discuss how the statement "Jesus is Lord" can be each of the following:

   A confession of faith

   A declaration of allegiance

   A sermon subject

   A shout of praise

5. Why did the Christian creeds get longer and more complex across the years?

6. Why did the lordship of Christ become more of a central theme in the creeds across the years?

7. If called on, would you have been willing to die for your faith in the early Christian persecutions?

8. How can you take the resolve and commitment of your response to question 7 and use it to live for Christ each day of your life?

PRACTICE THIS

1. List specific ways you can pass the faith of our fathers and mothers on to your children and grandchildren. What action steps will you begin today? This week?

2. Contemplate the words to the song "Made Up Mind," by Phillips, Craig, and Dean. Watch it on YouTube* if you are not

*"Made Up Mind—Phillips, Craig, and Dean," YouTube, http://www.youtube.com/watch?v=Dv4v6IZD3P8 (accessed April 22, 2013).

familiar with it. Reflect on how this idea will help you stand firm in your faith convictions when called on to do so.

3. In the span of one week, take note of how many songs and choruses you hear or sing with "Jesus is Lord" as the theme. How many did you total at the end of the week?

4. Take time to memorize the Apostles' Creed.

CHAPTER THREE

BEGINNING AT THE BEGINNING

There above it stood the

LORD, and he said: "I am the

LORD, the God of your father

Abraham and the God of

Isaac. I will give you and your

descendants the land on

which you are lying."

—God's word to Jacob
in Gen. 28:13

Most of us have a general idea of what the Bible means by lordship. But we find ourselves overwhelmed when we turn to the Bible for specific insights into the concept. There is so much material! How do we make sense of it all? Where do we even start?

The Greek version of the Old Testament, the Septuagint, used the word "lord" more than nine thousand times to refer to both God as Lord and humans as leaders of people. That's a lot of detail to process. So let's break it down into some simple, basic concepts to get a working definition of lordship.

The word "lord" is used in reference to God nearly two hundred times in the book of Genesis and in the first two chapters of Exodus. This gives us our first picture of God. The proper name for God in Genesis is *El Shaddai*, which is Hebrew for "God, the Mountain One." This could refer to God's great power or to the mountains as a symbol for his home. Either way, the name is rather generic and impersonal.[1] At best, followers of God in the Old Testament had a limited understanding of God's traits and personality. He seemed big and distant to them.

This began to change in Exodus as God gradually revealed more of himself to his children. God introduced himself to Moses at the burning bush in Exod. 3:14-15 with a new name. Here he called himself "I AM" (v. 14). The Hebrew word for "I AM" is *YHWH*. English requires us to add vowels, so we spell the name *Yahweh*. This is the most intimate and personal name used in the Old Testament for God—far more revealing than El Shaddai. The Hebrew people never pronounced the name Yahweh, because they revered it as too sacred to be uttered by human lips. They feared they might violate the biblical injunctions against misusing God's name: "You shall not misuse the name of the LORD your God, for the LORD will not hold anyone guiltless who misuses his name" (20:7). "Anyone who blasphemes the name of the LORD is to be put to death. The entire assembly must stone them. Whether foreigner or native-born, when they blaspheme the Name they are to be put to death" (Lev. 24:16).[2]

We in the church age call on the name of the Lord every day. We pronounce his name often. However, the ancient Hebrews remind us of an important spiritual truth: we must always maintain a reverent heart and say God's name with respect. We cannot let the irreverence of our age creep into our daily conversation so that we treat God disrespectfully.

Before we get too far into the story, let's stop and look further at God's Old Testament names.

Words Used

We just identified the Hebrew word *Yahweh*. We find it often translated into English as "Lord." Many Bibles print "Lord" in all capital letters (or large and small capitals). Some English translations, such as the King James Version, use the word "Jehovah" in references such as Exod. 6:3; Ps. 83:18; and Isa. 12:2; 26:4.[3] "Jehovah" is a spelling for the name of God that formed over time by joining the consonants of the next Hebrew word we will look at.[4]

This other Hebrew word for lord is *adon*. It literally refers to someone with absolute control, such as a master over slaves or a ruler over a group of people. The plural form of this word is *Adonai*. Scripture uses the plural form to distinguish a divine reference from a human one. The ending of God's name is in first-person, singular possessive and is translated "my Lord."[5] To show their reverence for God, whenever the Hebrew people saw the word *Yahweh* in Scripture, they said *Adonai*.[6] Yahweh (or Jehovah) and Adonai are the most common Old Testament names for God that signify his lordship over all.

Old Testament References

Exod. 3:14-15

Now let's return to Moses at the burning bush to see what new insight God revealed about himself to Moses in their encounter. He called himself "I AM WHO I AM" (v. 14). As we've seen, it's spelled "Yahweh" in English. In its various tenses, it means "I am," "I will be," "he is," and "he will be." Without getting too philosophical, let me just note here that God identified himself as the very source of being itself. The name Yahweh is based on the verb "to be" in Hebrew. Thus, Yahweh is the One Who Has Always Existed, that is, Being. Or to put it another way, he is the One Who Causes All Things to Come into Being. He is the Being who gives our being reality. Namely, because he exists, we can exist. Quite simply, our life flows from his.

From this point on in his dealings with humanity, God wished to be called by this more personal name. *I Am* is so much warmer than the *Powerful One Who Lives on the Mountain*. Linguistic scholars tell us that this name speaks of God's character as reliable and holy. Further, it tells us that our God reaches out to his children in mercy to redeem them—as he did in delivering his people from Egyptian bondage.[7] So this distant God who lived in the mountains, as noted in the early chapters of Genesis, pulled back the curtain and reached out to slaves in Egyptian bondage. He wanted to help them and show them mercy. He wanted to call them his children and to have them be in relationship with him!

Exod. 6:2-8

As Moses and his people moved into the early stages of the Exodus, God shared an interesting insight with Moses about his name. You might say God's progressive revelation about himself continued as he revealed a new image of who he is. The phrase "I am the LORD" appears four times in this passage. Make no mistake—God was in charge of their situation. He assured Moses that he was going to deliver them out of Egypt. His plan would not be defeated. They would one day live as free people after God brought them safely to their Promised Land.

God made an interesting observation to Moses in verse 3: "I appeared to Abraham, to Isaac and to Jacob as God Almighty, but by my name the LORD I did not make myself fully known to them."

This confirms what we said at the beginning of the chapter. God's followers prior to Moses knew him only by his generic and impersonal name. They did not know the name Yahweh—this God who is reliable, holy, full of mercy, and bringing deliverance. Not until the time of the Exodus did God's people recognize him as a God of redemption.[8]

In brief, God told Moses that he did not call himself "LORD" to the Genesis people. But we said that the word "lord" is used nearly two hundred times in Genesis as a reference to God. How is that? The problem here is that the Hebrew writer of Genesis used the name Yahweh to alert the reader that the God of the Exodus is the same God in Genesis. So even if the people depicted in Genesis didn't know the name, the writer who composed Genesis did.[9] As mentioned earlier, Yahweh is translated into English by capitalizing all the letters of the word "lord." So the word "lord" (all capitalized) is indeed used many times in both Genesis and Exodus to refer to Yahweh.[10] So, returning to Exod. 6:3, only to Moses—up to this point in salvation history—did God reveal himself as Yahweh, that is, God the Redeemer. What a wonderful revelation!

Men and Women Who Made God Lord of Their Lives

Abraham—Gen. 12:1-3; 17:1-6

God placed the life of Abraham in the Bible as an example of a man who followed and pleased him. To this very day—four thousand years later—Abraham's life shines as a beacon light, directing us to live a life that pleases God. In Isa. 41:8, God calls Abraham "my friend." That's an outstanding compliment. Abraham is the only Bible character to receive that description. Perhaps the greatest compliment a person can be paid is to be called a friend of God—especially when it comes from God himself!

Abraham's life was about as ordinary as any of ours. He had good days and bad, like the rest of us. Many people may think Abraham, as a Bible character, lived a glamorous life of spiritual stardom, filled with eventful days of glorious heavenly blessings. Not so! Most days he just scuffed his scandals through the hot, dry desert sand and minded his own business.

It appears that Abraham's most unique quality was his childlike faith to live for and trust God, one day at a time. Genesis 15:6 says, "Abram believed the Lord, and he credited it to him as righteousness." Paul repeated the same idea in Rom. 4:3. Believing God doesn't necessarily produce a glamorous lifestyle. Abraham had temptations and trials just as we do. Yet through it all, he chose to remain faithful and true to his Lord.

Genesis 17:1 contains God's special call to Abraham. God says to Abraham, "Walk before me faithfully and be blameless." Blameless. That's a powerful concept. Blameless does not imply perfect, as in free from mistakes. It pictures a person wholeheartedly seeking to do God's will. This is not about someone wanting God's will mixed with his or her own will. It's about having an undiluted desire to do what God wants. God finds such unmixed desire acceptable and characterizes such a life as blameless. Blameless is one of the key biblical signs of holiness in the human heart.

Bible scholars analyzing verse 1 often make an interesting observation. A casual reading of this verse seems to portray God giving Abraham a command: "Be blameless." However, scholars note that because Abraham's lifestyle, resolve, and heart are already totally focused on God, the phrase can be interpreted, not as an imperative or a command, but as a consequence. In other words, Abraham's daily walk with the Lord resulted in him being declared blameless by God. Wow! He walked before God in such a way that "every single step is made with reference to God and every day experiences him close at hand."[11] So God was not offering being blameless as a goal for which Abraham should strive; he was declaring that their daily walk together found Abraham blameless in God's eyes.

Abraham had certainly made his share of mistakes by this point in the story. He had lied to the Egyptian Pharaoh about Sarah being his wife (12:19). He and Sarah had frustrated God's plan for a child by having Hagar serve as a surrogate mother (16:3). We should note here that their actions were completely legitimate methods for growing a family according to the customs of their day. Their plan was not what God had in mind, however. Through Abraham's occasional errors in judgment, he sought wholeheartedly to find and do God's will.[12] When he stumbled, he didn't wallow in his mistakes. Rather, he sought God's guidance, got back up, and started again. Abraham is a good example for us in this way.

Here's what interests me most about Abraham's spiritual journey. He came early in the Genesis story, so he got in on the beginning of God's revelation of himself to humanity. Yet he lived this exemplary life with such limited knowledge about our God. Even with limited understanding, he made God Lord of his life. Those of us who live in the church age know Jesus Christ personally. We have the Holy Spirit living within our hearts; we have so many more spiritual resources available to us than Abraham had.

It's a haunting question for us. How much more should we make this personal, merciful God Lord of our lives? Abraham made God Lord over all of his life while working with such limited resources. His story is an inspiration to us to take the incredible resources Jesus Christ has made available to us through the power of the Holy Spirit and make him Lord over all our lives.

King Saul—1 Sam. 10–31

We always notice firsts—the first customer in a new store, the first dollar spent, the first student enrolled in a new school, the first car to drive on a new road, and so on. Firsts are usually a big deal. This is certainly the case with Israel's first king. The people of Israel begged the Lord through his prophet Samuel for a king so they could be like neighboring nations. God reluctantly granted their request and selected Saul, the son of Kish. He had everything the people sought in a king: height, strong build, military ability, humility, and pleasing personality.

God's Spirit filled Saul for his new role (10:10). In the beginning Saul made all of the right moves. He seemed to have a good relationship with his God. Throughout the life story of King Saul recorded in 1 Sam. 10–31, Saul called on the name of the Lord many times, prophesied in his name, sought his advice, and worshipped him regularly.

And yet, the Bible records no more tragic a failure than the relationship Saul had with his Lord. So where did Saul go wrong? We need to carefully analyze Saul's spiritual journey to see if we can pinpoint early signs of slippage long before the actual crisis that signaled the rupture in his spiritual relationship. If we can pinpoint those early signs, perhaps we can learn valuable lessons for our own spiritual journey.

The root of the problem seemed to spring up early in Saul's career. As I said, he started out humbly enough. Read 1 Sam. 10:22 for an example of his humility. "So they inquired further of the LORD, 'Has the man come here yet?' And the LORD said, 'Yes, he has hidden himself among the supplies.'" The prophet Samuel was trying to locate Saul to anoint him the first king of Israel, but Saul hid himself. They found him hiding shyly in a closet. Then later, as we will soon see, Saul began to shift away from a posture of humbly waiting for the Lord to act in his life.

What factors contributed to Saul's shift in spiritual priority is uncertain. Perhaps all of the attention, fame, honor, and privilege of being king went to his head. Perhaps he enjoyed having people serve him. Perhaps his military and political power made him proud and self-important. Such accolades often have a tendency to affect leaders in negative ways. For whatever reason, the story of Saul irreverently performing a religious ceremony in 13:5-14 indicates that he was just going through the motions of worship so he could get it behind him and get on with a battle. It's almost as though he was thinking, *Yeah, yeah, whatever. Let's get this worship thing over with. We have a battle to fight. The preacher is late; I'm a busy man. I can't be kept waiting.*

Saul again betrayed his relationship with his Lord in 15:1-35. Perhaps God could have restored Saul to a place of spiritual leadership if he would have shown a contrite spirit after his blunder recorded in 13:5-14. But the incident recorded in chapter 15 indicates spiritual problems on multiple levels. In fact, Saul's sin mirrors Achan's sin recorded in Josh. 7:1-26, which resulted in Achan's execution. They both disobeyed God and lied about it. God did not execute Saul on this occasion, but he did pass serious judgment on him. Saul's spirituality had reached an all-time low. His betrayal led Samuel to utter some of the most powerful words in the entire Old Testament— words that capture the heart of God's desire for all of his children. Samuel said to Saul as he rejected him as king of Israel, "Does the LORD delight in burnt offerings and sacrifices as much as in obeying the LORD? To obey is better than sacrifice, and to heed is better than the fat of rams" (1 Sam. 15:22). This verse offers a very simple message. God values an obedient relationship with his children more than he values their performance of religious acts and utterance of pious words.

As in the previous example, Saul performed the religious ritual flawlessly. He went through the motions, he said the proper words, and he made the sacrifice. His problem? He had no relationship with his Lord. The communication lines were down; the connection broken. We even have a hint in the story that Saul was more concerned with preserving his personal image before the elders than he was in fixing his broken relationship with his Lord. "Saul replied, 'I have sinned. But please honor me before the elders of my people and before Israel; come back with me, so that I may worship the LORD your God'" (v. 30). He wanted the prophet to help him protect his public image.

Here are two additional thoughts about Saul's failure. Verse 13 indicates that Saul was in big trouble with the Lord and didn't even know it. Saul hoped God would accept his religious performance with a big smile on his face. We occupy a dangerous place when we slip away from the presence of the Lord, fall into sin, and remain oblivious to our plight. First Samuel 16:14 says, "The Spirit of the LORD had departed from Saul." In other words, he lost the Lord's special blessing on his life—a blessing he needed to lead the nation successfully. Yet he continued to occupy the throne for many more years. Here again, we occupy a dangerous place when we continue to go through the motions of religious performance if the Spirit of the Lord no longer fills and blesses us.

The spiritual life and failures of King Saul offer us some sobering reminders. These reminders focus our attention on lordship issues for our own lives:

- Just like Saul, we need the Lord's presence and blessing for success in life.
- Just like Saul, temptations to compromise will always knock at our door.
- Just like Saul, we can go through the motions; only we and the Lord will know the true condition of our heart.
- Just like Saul, we can keep up the image for many years without peace of mind.
- Just like Saul, if we do not make God Lord of all, our lives will spin out of control and end in spiritual tragedy.

All of these sobering reminders come from a man who had so much promise. God never intended his life to end the way it did. God never intends that end for any of us, either.

King David—1 Sam. 16–1 Kings 2:11

The brightest spot in Israel's political, religious, and literary history shines from the life of King David. We remember David as one of the most prominent figures in the history of the world, one of the most notable Bible characters, and the most famous ancestor of our Lord Jesus Christ. Isn't it interesting that we call Jesus the Son of David, not the Son of Abraham, Isaac, or Jacob?

David's life was a blend of good and evil. He wrote Ps. 23 and had Uriah killed. He accomplished noble deeds and had high aspirations.

He rose victorious over many temptations but succumbed to others. We could focus on his ability in athletics, music, literature, warfare, administration, or leadership. But instead, we will turn our attention to a different area of his life. We will concentrate on David's personal relationship with his Lord.

David began his career humbly before his God much as Saul did. God chose him as the least of his fellow Israelites, his tribe, and his family. Neither Samuel nor David's father, Jesse, saw the leadership potential in David that God saw (1 Sam. 16:1-12). God worked quietly behind the scenes preparing David for the roles he would later serve (vv. 13, 17-18). It's especially intriguing that David waited many years on God's timing and leadership. He did not assume actual authority as king when the Lord—through Samuel's ministry—anointed him as the next king of Israel after having rejected Saul's leadership. Instead, David had to wait a long time. What does that say to us about letting God be Lord over our situations? It may take God years to move all of the pieces into their proper places. Can we patiently wait on his timing as David did?

The book of Psalms offers us a treasure chest of insights into David's relationship with his Lord. These songs reveal David at his best and at his worst. David penned these songs on good days and bad. We see him climbing to the top of spiritual mountains and falling into the depths of spiritual valleys. Yet, through it all, we see a firm resolve to keep the Lord fully in control of his life. That's an important word: "resolve." Don't forget it. It's one of David's lessons on lordship for us.

Here are just a few examples of David's spiritual thoughts put to song:

Praise

Praise the LORD, my soul;
>   all my inmost being, praise his holy name.
Praise the LORD, my soul,
>   and forget not all his benefits—

who forgives all your sins
    and heals all your diseases,
who redeems your life from the pit
    and crowns you with love and compassion,
who satisfies your desires with good things
    so that your youth is renewed like the eagle's. (103:1-5)

Worship

I rejoiced with those who said to me,
    "Let us go to the house of the LORD." (122:1)

Conversion

I waited patiently for the LORD;
    he turned to me and heard my cry.
He lifted me out of the slimy pit,
    out of the mud and mire;
he set my feet on a rock
    and gave me a firm place to stand.
He put a new song in my mouth,
    a hymn of praise to our God.
Many will see and fear the LORD
    and put their trust in him.
Blessed is the one
    who trusts in the LORD,
who does not look to the proud,
    to those who turn aside to false gods. (40:1-4)

Pardon

Blessed is the one
    whose transgressions are forgiven,
    whose sins are covered.
Blessed is the one
    whose sin the LORD does not count against them
    and in whose spirit is no deceit. (32:1-2)

Perhaps the most complimentary words God could say about any of us, he said of David: "a man after his own heart" (1 Sam. 13:14). How do we reconcile this compliment with David's many shortcomings, failures, and sins? The likely answer is that even though David did not always get it right, and even though he failed miserably at times, (1) he maintained a humble attitude, (2) he ran back quickly to God, and (3) he trusted the Lord to forgive and restore him. To his credit, David always responded in contrition when confronted by God's prophetic voice (2 Sam. 12). No better example of this can be found than the words of Ps. 51—words penned after his adulterous affair with Bathsheba.

> Have mercy on me, O God,
>> according to your unfailing love;
> according to your great compassion
>> blot out my transgressions.
> Wash away all my iniquity
>> and cleanse me from my sin.
> For I know my transgressions,
>> and my sin is always before me.
> Against you, you only, have I sinned
>> and done what is evil in your sight;
> so you are right in your verdict
>> and justified when you judge. . . .
> Yet you desired faithfulness even in the womb;
>> you taught me wisdom in that secret place.
> Cleanse me with hyssop, and I will be clean;
>> wash me, and I will be whiter than snow.
> Let me hear joy and gladness;
>> let the bones you have crushed rejoice.
> Hide your face from my sins
>> and blot out all my iniquity.
> Create in me a pure heart, O God,
>> and renew a steadfast spirit within me.

Do not cast me from your presence

    or take your Holy Spirit from me.

Restore to me the joy of your salvation

    and grant me a willing spirit, to sustain me. (Vv. 1-4, 6-12)

The reminder from David's life is that though he failed, he came back in humble repentance and reaffirmed or restored his relationship with the Lord. He did not let pride get in his way. He did not let power go to his head. He did not let failure define him. Many great things have been said about David across the years, but perhaps the best is that he was "a man after [God's] own heart" (1 Sam. 13:14). May it be so of each of us.

Elijah—1 Kings 18:16-46

We often lament that we must serve Jesus Christ in an age of religious pluralism. So many other gods receive worship and praise in our land these days. The environment of our politically correct climate places Jesus on an equal playing field with these other gods. It's like the bumper sticker that says, "One God; many paths." Our society urges us not only to remain open-minded and tolerant toward these other world religions but also to embrace their views as equally valid and true with ours. "All religions are filled with truth," we are told. "We must respect and honor them all."

When you encounter the frustration of religious pluralism, take heart. We are not the first generation of people to face this challenge. God's people have faced it throughout time. One example of a believer facing this challenge occurred during the ministry of Elijah. He had a face-to-face showdown with the priests of Baal and Asherah (v. 19). In Canaanite religion, Asherah, Ashtoreth, and Anath were the three great Canaanite goddesses (sometimes identified with each other). If you haven't read the passage in a while, take a few minutes and read 1 Kings 18:16-46. It's a fascinating story of a religious pluralism face-off.

Now that you've refreshed your mind with the story, let's look at it more carefully. Notice first that religious pluralism plagued the land in Elijah's day, just as we face it today. God raised up the Hebrew people to be his people. They had specific instructions from God to worship only him. At different times and in an almost infinite variety of ways, they strayed from that instruction. This passage of Scripture highlights just one of those times. It is also noteworthy that the contest between Elijah and the priests of Baal took place on Mount Carmel. That gave the Baal priests the "home court advantage," since Mount Carmel served as a center for Baal worship.

The word *baal* translates into English as "lord." Baal was the principal male god of the Phoenicians. The plural *baalim* (lords) occurs several places in the Bible.[13] The Hebrew people at different times in their history worshipped Baal, along with Yahweh, until Yahweh finally put a stop to it with the severe discipline of the captivity (Zeph. 1:4-6). First Kings 18:16-46 tells us not only about these priests but also about their mode of offering sacrifices. The sun-god, also called Baal, was the chief object of worship of the Canaanites, the Hebrews' neighbors.[14]

Asherah, or the plural Asherim, was the name of a sensual Canaanite goddess. God's people brought the worship of this goddess into their community along with the worship of Baal. This religion is most noted for its popular symbol—a tree branch shaped into the form of a male reproductive organ. They also used silver or stone to form this image.[15] These symbols were then planted in the ground in groups known as groves. This is the reason the Asherah poles are often referred to as groves in the Bible.[16]

Elijah found himself a spiritual stranger in his own homeland the day he put the priests of Baal and Asherah to the test. Both the Elijah and Elisha narratives in Scripture serve as a polemic against Baal worship. These prophets and their ministries demonstrated that Yahweh is superior in every way. Elijah asked a powerful question on the day of the test that rings true today. "How long will you waver between two opinions? If the LORD is God, follow him; but if Baal is God, follow him" (1 Kings 18:21). Over and over again the Bible reminds us that we were not created to serve many lords. We must make our choice and concentrate all of our efforts on the worship of just one lord.

When we read this old story, we're tempted to think that Baal worship reflects a story long ago and far away. Not so! Baal worship remains as current as this morning's newspaper. You see, Satan recycles, repackaging old sins in new forms for each new generation. People fall into these old traps thinking they have found their way into practices new and exciting.[17] It's like the recycling of clothing styles from one decade to the next. So-called new styles today are just variations of styles that were worn years before.

This story from the ministry of Elijah has many powerful spiritual insights. We don't have space to explore them here. But what is most important for our purposes is that this event reminds us to be intentional about whom we call Lord. We must make a conscious decision and then live it. Elijah was not outwitted, and we don't have to be either. The world has many lords to offer us. Remember that every day. We can be victorious in this world of religious pluralism. If we do not take great care, we might just find ourselves giving our allegiance to Baal without realizing it. But also remember, we don't have to do that. We can be victorious!

Elijah is correct. We cannot serve two lords. Our Creator wired us to serve only one. So we must choose purposefully. What an example of making God Lord over all of life in the midst of open opposition!

Special Women in the Old Testament

We will balance the four men of the Old Testament with four women who illustrate, in different ways, their allegiance to their Lord. The Old Testament offers many fine examples of women who excelled in their commitment to their God. How do we choose just four? Perhaps the easiest way out of the dilemma is to let God choose four women from the Old Testament. "How do you do that?" you ask.

We will choose the four women included in the genealogy of Jesus in Matt. 1:1-17. The presence of women in this genealogy is highly significant, because a Jewish lineage did not normally list women. A woman was nothing more than a man's property—like his donkey or his tent. Women had no status in the culture of that day. They had no importance or legal rights. Society did not even give them personhood outside of their being wives of men and mothers of children. Jewish men would pray the following prayer every day: "Lord, I thank you that I am not a Gentile, a slave, or a woman."[18]

The fact that Jesus' lineage contains four women is outrageous enough. What's worse, look who they were! They all have social or moral stigmas attached to them.

• Rahab earned her living as an innkeeper and a prostitute in Jericho several years after God's chosen people had made their exodus from Egyptian bondage. By the time the Hebrews reached Jericho, they had been kicking desert sand for about forty years. Then Joshua sent two spies on a reconnaissance mission into the city. Rahab figured out what the spies were doing and hid them. She may have anticipated what God was about to do for his people. You can read the story in Josh. 2:1-24. She accepted the God of the Hebrews and wanted to be part of what God was doing for his special people. God forgave her of her sins. He took her back from her life of prostitution and, of all things, made her a grandmother of Jesus! Now, that's true forgiveness! She made God Lord of her life as she joined the Hebrew people.

• Ruth, like Rahab, was not a Hebrew woman. She was a Moabite (Ruth 1:4). The Moabites lived in a neighboring nation and were condemned by Hebrew law; they were a hated and alien people. Think of them as the neighbors who lived on the other side of town who nobody liked and nobody had anything to do with. And they sure didn't let their children date Moabite children!

But Ruth dated a Hebrew man and married him. Yes, he had broken Hebrew custom while living out of the homeland. After he died, his widow, Ruth, returned to the Hebrew Promised Land with her mother-in-law, Naomi. Ruth accepted the Hebrew people's God, and God accepted her. He took her in as a foreigner and made her a grandmother of Jesus! Now that's true adoption! She made God Lord of her life as she joined the Hebrew people. Her declaration of allegiance to Naomi is often read at weddings today: "Where you go I will go, and where you stay I will stay. Your people will be my people and your God my God" (v. 16).

• Tamar had a life story that would make any Hollywood movie producer blush. She was a member of the dysfunctional family of one of Jacob's sons. You can read her story in Gen. 38. It's difficult for modern readers to comprehend exactly what is happening, because the soap opera story line is filled with ancient Middle Eastern social and ethical laws of obligation. We do not have rules with which to compare these laws today, so a brief explanation is in order.

Judah, Tamar's father-in-law, failed to provide for her future care when his son, her husband, died. She took matters into her own hands and seduced Judah for children and to secure her future. Were her actions wrong? According to today's moral standards they were; Judah, however, said she was more right than he was according to the ethical obligations of that day (v. 26). She seduced her father-in-law and became the family outcast for her actions. But Gen. 38 is not the final chapter of the story. Matthew informs us that God apparently forgave her. He took her back from her life of adultery and made her a grandmother of Jesus! With the details known only to God, he became her Lord.

• Bathsheba committed adultery with King David when she involved herself in a love triangle. David decided "three is a crowd," so he had her husband, Uriah, killed (2 Sam. 11–12). This is another one of those Bible soap opera stories! We have already discussed David's side of the story earlier in the chapter and read his prayer of confession for this sin in Ps. 51.

We are here again dealing with ancient Middle Eastern mores, so we find ourselves at a disadvantage in analyzing just how much moral blame Bathsheba held in this situation. Was she morally obligated to do the king's bidding? Or did she enjoy his carnal attention. Perhaps only she knew the answers to those questions. We do know she prospered from her interactions with David (1 Kings 2:19). We also know that whatever level of blame she may have had, like David, God forgave her. He took her back from her adultery and then made her a grandmother of Jesus! Now, that's gracious forgiveness! She made God Lord of her life and became, from that point on, an example for us.

Conclusion

We live in a world of Facebook, Google, Skype, cell phones, instant messaging, and texting. We think we're a sophisticated and highly advanced civilization. By the way, people thought the same thing one hundred years ago too! We read ancient stories from the Old Testament and think, *What could those people of the Middle Eastern desert possibly teach me, anyway?*

As we have seen from this brief overview, God revealed himself to humanity progressively across the years. He pulled the curtain back a little at a time. It seems that as our comprehension of him grew, he revealed more of himself to us. One thing is for sure: from the opening moments of humanity's time on earth, God never left himself without a witness. First through creation, then through his name, God told us about himself.

We learn amazing things about our God just by analyzing his name. People down through all the ages of the Old Testament learned about God from the various ways he revealed himself to them. Many of them made him Lord of their lives. The Bible highlights a few of their stories as inspirational examples for us. The Bible provides full-color details in these stories. It does not airbrush out the blemishes, mistakes, or flaws in these people's lives. Why? Because God wants us to learn from their mistakes and hopefully not make them again.

The time may be long ago, and the land may be far away. However, we can learn much about lordship from these Old Testament pilgrims.

THINK ABOUT THIS

1. What did you learn about the progressive revelation of God as he presented more of himself to us through his various names in the Old Testament?

2. What spiritual life lesson do you learn from Abraham?

3. What spiritual life lesson do you learn from King Saul?

4. What spiritual life lesson do you learn from King David?

5. What spiritual life lesson do you learn from Elijah?

6. What do you learn about God from the way he adopted Rahab, Ruth, Tamar, and Bathsheba as the grandmothers of Jesus?

PRACTICE THIS

1. For a day, put yourself in the sandals of Abraham and Sarah. Imagine that you know little about God other than that he created everything and that he promised to guide you. How do you live your life differently with this limited understanding of God? How do you relate to God differently with this limited understanding of him?

2. For a day, put yourself in the sandals of Elijah, with the priests of Baal and Asherah in control of the land. What will you do to get your friends to understand your faith that Jesus is Lord when these other voices are so dominant? (By the way, our world is not that different from Elijah's, so the circumstances in this exercise could easily happen in real life.)

3. Whatever your situation is today, write one of David's songs or prayers that fits it. Personalize the song or prayer by writing it using personal pronouns and your name. Read it back to yourself, and hear the message from God to you.

4. Think of a person in your life and reflect on how that person strayed from God but then came back to God with a repentant heart and spirit. Think of another person you might reach and help bring back to God as well.

CHAPTER FOUR

HEAVEN TO EARTH

That at the name of Jesus

every knee should bow, in

heaven and on earth and under

the earth, and every tongue

acknowledge that Jesus Christ

is Lord, to the glory of God

the Father.

—Phil. 2:10-11

The New Testament tells us the good news about the God-man sent by the Father to live among us. The very name Christ Jesus points to his duel nature: "Christ" speaks to his divinity, while "Jesus" reminds us of his humanity. Something about this One who lived among us for such a short time changed everything about life for us on earth forever. His earthly life, death, resurrection from the dead, and ascension back to the Father brought us the possibility to live differently. We now have a new perspective and a new purpose. That's how much the lordship of Christ changed everything for us.

A book on the lordship of Christ would not have found a wide audience a few years ago. Most of us placed much of our confidence in science and technology. We thought with enough time and research the twin lords could solve all of the problems that plagued humanity. We just had to keep funding the research and waiting for the breakthroughs. We put our trust in what we could see, taste, touch, count, and analyze. Scientists told us that time spent with anything other than the scientifically observable was wasted. Unfortunately, we believed them.

Those days have passed. We now realize that science and technology promised more than they could deliver. Their discoveries brought us drugs with side effects worse than our illnesses; they brought us new problems as complex as the ones they solved. So maybe they are not lords worthy of our allegiance after all.

Maybe we need to search for meaning in life that goes beyond what we can see, taste, touch, count, and analyze. Maybe the life example and teachings of Christ Jesus have something to say to us in the twenty-first century. And maybe, just maybe, that blessed name of Jesus offers the peace that our longing hearts seek.

Greek Words Used in the New Testament

Remember the Old Testament Hebrew words used most often for Lord? *Yahweh* and *Adonai*. Greek served as the language of the New Testament. Both *Yahweh* and *Adonai* translated into Greek as *Kyrios*.

The word literally means "supreme master."[1] Most of the time the word references God the Father or Christ the Son, although sometimes it occurs with reference to anyone in authority over people. For example, Jesus used the term in describing the shrewd manager in Luke 16:1-15. Paul used the term in describing the relationship between masters and slaves in Eph. 6:5-9.[2]

In chapter 3 we noted that the Greek version of the Old Testament used the word "lord" more than nine thousand times. The task of sorting through the rich nuances of meaning for our God as Lord proved to be daunting. We can study its rich meaning for the rest of our lives. We have our work cut out for us as we approach the New Testament as well. The Greek word *kyrios*, usually translated as "master" or "lord," occurs 717 times in the New Testament. Luke used the word 210 times; Paul used it even more, at 275 times.

People used the term "lord" in several different ways in reference to Jesus Christ during his earthly ministry. The crowds listening to his sermons often called him Lord as a respectful title they offered to a rabbi or Jewish teacher of the Law. Upon seeing Jesus transfigured before him by the Father, Peter used the term to indicate Jesus was both a respected teacher and highly exalted by God in this special way. "Peter said to Jesus, 'Lord, it is good for us to be here'" (Matt. 17:4a).

Jesus accepted the respectful use of the term "lord" during his public ministry. However, in Luke 6:46-49 he appeared frustrated that his listeners were quick to call him Lord but slow to put that understanding to work in their personal lives. How was it that they could so quickly recognize who he was but could not immediately apply it?

He then offered the insightful parable of the wise and foolish builders. The wise builder dug down deep and set a solid foundation on bedrock for the house he built. The foolish builder constructed his house at ground level, without care for a solid foundation.

The first builder represented those who put Jesus' words into practice in their lives; the second one represented those who gave verbal assent to his message but never got around to applying it. Jesus seemed to be saying, "If you are going to call me Lord, live like it. Otherwise, don't bother!"[3]

From the very heart of Jesus himself, we see that lordship is never a casual matter. He expects us to decide if we want to make him Lord of our lives. Then if we reach that decision, we should pour all our life's energy into living it out daily.

The Ultimate Validation

Use of the word "lord" in reference to Jesus Christ took on a different tone once Jesus was raised from the dead. After the resurrection, the term implied much more than respect for a teacher of the Law. As a result of that incredible event, the term now carried overtones of worship and exaltation from subjects to their divine leader. That's why the slogan "Jesus is Lord" troubled the Roman officials so much. As Christians spread the phrase across the Roman Empire, it spoke of their allegiance to the Risen Lord.[4]

Certainly the Roman officials did not consider Jesus as divine; they refused to even acknowledge his resurrection. The sticking point for them, as Christianity permeated the empire, was this issue of lordship. Christians refused to honor Caesar as Lord. They regarded the humble Jewish teacher Jesus as the Christ, the Messiah—the Sovereign Ruler of the universe.

That's a major shift in status! Yes, this shift in the thinking of Christ's followers gives us a peek at just how much his resurrection affected their understanding of him. The resurrection changed everything forever, both on earth and in heaven. Paul offered an interesting insight in 1 Cor. 8:5-6. He first acknowledged that many people use the term "lord" in reference to political leaders or pagan gods. They say, for example, "Caesar is Lord" or "Zeus is Lord." Most of us would be ready to jump into a heated debate over the use of the term—but not Paul. No, Paul refused to quarrel with people over the lordship issue. For him the matter was settled. He wanted his readers to understand that as far as he was concerned only One truly deserved that title. "Yet for us there is but one God, the Father, from whom all things came and for whom we live; and there is but one Lord, Jesus Christ" (v. 6). "Others can make the claim," Paul argued, "but only Jesus deserves to be called Lord!"

For the early church, the highest and best use of the word "lord," as they read their Bibles (i.e., the Old Testament), was in reference to God, Yahweh, Jehovah—that is, the Deity. So when they decided to apply this term equally to Jesus, they were letting the world know that they also acknowledged Jesus as the Deity. He, for them, was none other than the divine Son of God. It was no obscure or occasional reference to the idea, either. That's the reason for the special designation Lord Jesus Christ, which was used 274 times in the *New International Version* of the New Testament.

When most people hear the name Jesus Christ, they think of it as a first and last name. This is not the case for the early church. For the church, the name meant "Jesus who is the Christ" or "Jesus who is the Messiah." Even though we Christians commonly think of this as a double name for God's Son, we need to stop from time to time and remind ourselves that when we say the name Jesus Christ, we are making a faith statement: "Jesus is our Christ—our Messiah."[5]

Two practices caught on quickly in the early Christian church to constantly remind Christ's followers of his lordship and divine status: the Lord's Day and the Lord's Supper. The Lord's Day shifted worship of God from the last day of the week, as it had been in Jewish tradition, to the first day of the week. Sunday's celebration reminded believers every week that Jesus was raised from the dead on that day and now sits at the right hand of the Father. The Lord's Supper reminded believers of the high price Jesus paid for their salvation in his sacrificial death on the cross. It further reminded them that they had new spiritual life in him through the power of the Holy Spirit.[6] These two frequent reminders have affirmed the lordship of Christ in Christian tradition from the early days of the church until now.

New Testament References

John 1:47-51

Jesus' disciples were given profound insight into recognizing his uniqueness, even as he called them into his service. Early in Jesus' ministry, Nathanael's confession, "Rabbi, you are the Son of God; you are the king of Israel" (v. 49), alerts us to the Spirit of God opening Nathanael's eyes to perceive Jesus as the Christ. In his encounter with Nathanael, Jesus made a passing reference to Jacob's vision of God's angels on a ladder between heaven and earth. He identified himself as the Son of Man—a title that spoke to his lordship. Jesus dropped hints, like this one, about his divinity throughout his ministry.[7] It's exciting to read and reread the gospel accounts to find clues to his lordship.

Jesus used the title Son of Man numerous times throughout his earthly ministry. The title connected his humanity to his divinity, since it came from Daniel's vision of the four beasts, as recorded in Dan. 7:1-14. In this vision, Daniel saw the authority, glory, and sovereign power given to the Son of Man so that he can rule as Lord over all creation. Jesus used this title in such a way that his hearers had to decide for themselves if they wanted to accept his lordship. He implied that he brought salvation through his ministry if his hearers wanted to receive him as their Lord.[8] He made the case but left it up to them to decide. Some chose to follow him; others did not.

Luke 7:11-17

The story of Jesus raising a widow's son from the dead in Luke 7 offers an interesting shift in thinking. Prior to verse 13, his followers called him Lord in the sense of a respected teacher (see 5:8, 12) or as One who had jurisdiction over the Sabbath (see 6:5). However, in 7:13 Luke refers to him as Lord with a reverence reserved for God the Father alone. This important shift in the use of the word "lord" signals a major transition in Jesus' ministry.

Here we find in *Kyrios* (Lord) a Greek translation of the name Yahweh—God of the Old Testament. Jesus' ability to raise this young man from the dead signaled to the crowd, as well as his followers, that his power could only be explained by the phrase, "God has come to help his people" (v. 16). Something beyond explanation had happened in their midst that day. Now when they called Jesus Lord, they did so with the awareness that he could even raise the dead.[9]

Matt. 16:13-20

Though the word "lord" is not used, no study of the lordship of Christ in the New Testament could be complete without a consideration of Peter's confession at Caesarea Philippi. This confession divides the entire gospel story of Jesus into two parts. Everything that Jesus said and did up to that time pointed to that moment. Peter confessed on the mountain in no uncertain terms the lordship of Christ: "You are the Messiah, the Son of the living God" (v. 16).

Peter was not speculating, hoping, or suggesting. He was declaring with certainty, "You are." Only the Spirit of God could have given him this understanding and insight. This beautiful insight does not point us to Peter's human faith but to God's divine purpose in sending Jesus to live with us. No doubt, Peter did not fully understand what Jesus' lordship would mean in the days ahead. That is, he did not grasp the meaning of Jesus' crucifixion, death, and resurrection. Nevertheless, the Father gave Peter a brief glimpse into the unique character of Jesus Christ the Lord.[10]

Phil. 2:5-11

Perhaps the most profound reference to Jesus Christ as Lord in the New Testament comes from the pen of Paul in Phil. 2. We must read it again before we begin to unpack the rich message found in this powerful message.

In your relationships with one another, have the same mindset as Christ Jesus:

Who, being in very nature God,

did not consider equality with God something to be used to
   his own advantage;
rather, he made himself nothing
   by taking the very nature of a servant,
   being made in human likeness.
And being found in appearance as a man,
   he humbled himself
   by becoming obedient to death—
      even death on a cross!
Therefore God exalted him to the highest place
   and gave him the name that is above every name,
that at the name of Jesus every knee should bow,
   in heaven and on earth and under the earth,
and every tongue acknowledge that Jesus Christ is Lord,
   to the glory of God the Father. (Vv. 5-11)

Paul provided in this short passage one of the most profound snapshots of God's plan of salvation recorded in Scripture. He took us to the mountaintop and showed us the grand sweep of God's majestic provision. He understood clearly that Jesus came down from heaven to earth with the express purpose of living among us, teaching us about the Father, giving us an example of righteousness to follow, going to the cross for our sins, dying on that cross, descending into the place of the dead, rising from the dead, and ascending back to the Father. He fulfilled that purpose right down to the smallest detail. As a result of his faithfulness, the Father rewarded him on his return to heaven with the distinguished title of Lord. It is that exaltation—"Jesus Christ is Lord"—that every person who has ever lived on this earth will bow and confess "to the glory of God the Father" at the end of time (v. 11).

This powerful passage of Scripture, which many believe circulated as an early Christian hymn used during worship services, is both a confession of faith in Christ's saving work and a confidence in God for a just conclusion to all earthly things. We also see in this passage both the humiliation of Christ and his exaltation. Again, it affirms his saving work on this earth and his glorification in heaven.

This passage thus serves as a historical statement and a shout of praise in worship to God. Adoration and acclamation belong to only one Lord—Jesus Christ. He is both Lord of the church and Lord of his entire creation.[11] He deserves to receive glory, honor, and devotion from the church and all citizens of the world.

Paul implied in this passage that the Holy Spirit came to live within believers when Jesus returned to the Father. In 1 Cor. 12:3, Paul reminded us that "no one can say, 'Jesus is Lord,' except by the Holy Spirit." So everyone on earth who freely confesses Jesus as Lord does so as he or she is enabled by the power of the Holy Spirit.[12]

1 Cor. 6:11

The early church also made reference to Jesus Christ as Lord when they baptized believers. In this verse from 1 Corinthians, Paul reminded the Corinthian Christians, "You were washed, you were sanctified, you were justified in the name of the Lord Jesus Christ and by the Spirit of our God." The verbs used here give strong indication that the one who performed the rite of baptism pronounced this statement of faith over the one being baptized. Although we do not know the exact wording of the baptismal formula, we do know that emphasis was placed on the affirmation of faith that Jesus Christ is Lord.[13]

1 Cor. 1:10

In this earlier verse from 1 Corinthians, Paul used the name of the Lord Jesus Christ in yet another way, when he said, "I appeal to you, brothers and sisters, in the name of our Lord Jesus Christ, that all of you agree with one another in what you say and that there be no divisions among you, but that you be perfectly united in mind and thought." A technical analysis of the original language yields the understanding that in this verse Paul was not attempting to remind his readers of the name of the Lord Jesus Christ. Rather, the structure of the sentence indicates that he was appealing to their relationship with Jesus as believers.[14]

With this in mind, Paul admonished his readers that since they have a relationship with Jesus Christ, they should agree with one another. The use of the title Lord here appeals to their divine-human relationship. You might at first think that this interpretation takes us out of the realm of worship, which is how we usually interpret our thinking of Christ Jesus as Lord. Not so. A peaceful relationship with other believers, or with nonbelievers, can, in fact, be an act of worship to God. One way we show love to God is by the way we love and get along with one another. Making Jesus Lord of our lives goes a long way in helping us organize all of our relationships with one another.

Men and Women Who Made Jesus Lord of Their Lives

Mary

Mary holds a unique place in Christian history. For as far back as we can recount in Jewish tradition, the Jews had awaited the coming of the Messiah. Every young Jewish girl hoped that she might be the chosen one to bear this long-awaited Redeemer. Then one day, without fanfare, the angel Gabriel appeared to Mary as an unwed teenager and announced that God had chosen her to be the mother of his prophesied Messiah (Luke 1:35).

She didn't really know what to make of the news. But then, who would? How do you explain such a message to your parents? We live in a time when unwed teens in many societies of our world can have babies and keep them without enduring social or moral stigmas. But that was not the case in Mary's day. She could have been stoned to death for her pregnancy. We can only guess beyond the silence of Scripture, but logic seems to suggest that Joseph defended her reputation to the townspeople. All of that to say, from the first day she learned about her connection to Jesus, Mary soon realized that identifying with him would cost her much.

The Bible does not tell us a great deal about Mary's personal life. We know she was from the tribe of Judah and the lineage of David. She lived in Nazareth and had agreed to marry Joseph before Gabriel appeared to her and turned her world upside down. Her cousin Elizabeth confirmed that God was using her to bring the Messiah to earth (vv. 41-45). Gabriel's visit and the testimony of Elizabeth, along with the angel's appearance to Joseph in a dream (Matt. 1:18-25), convinced the couple that God was orchestrating the birth of this special child who was to be the long-awaited Messiah.

Although Mary had the Lord's favor and received the designation mother of Jesus, her life did not become easy or privileged. Far from it! She bore the ridicule of the townspeople. As the men conducted village business and the women drew water at the community well, their tongues were wagging: "Did you hear? Mary's pregnant. She and Joseph haven't married yet. . . . What a shame!" She walked and rode a donkey while she was nine months pregnant, traveling ninety miles from Nazareth to Bethlehem to take part in the census decreed by the emperor (Luke 2:1). She had to settle for the only accommodations Joseph could find once they reached their destination—a livestock cave behind the inn.

Then she lay on the bed of hay, exhausted from her long journey. She thought about all they had been through over the past nine months and how their lives had radically changed. She might have even thought, *What else could go wrong today?* Then her labor began! Right there in the cave, in a strange town, with no mother or midwife to assist, with livestock looking on, she gave birth to our Savior.

Now that showed a willingness to let God be Lord of a situation that seemed totally out of control. But Mary was willing not only that night but from that point on. She and Joseph had to escape to Egypt for a couple of years to protect Jesus from King Herod's slaughter of the innocents, recorded in Matt. 2:13-18. We don't know much about her role in the years that followed, other than that she did a good job raising Jesus in the Jewish religious tradition. We catch a brief glimpse of Mary with Jesus at the temple when he was twelve years old talking with the scholars (Luke 2:41-52).

Once Jesus began his public ministry, we see Mary at the marriage in Cana. Interestingly, she seemed to have a mother's persuasive influence over the Son of God. He had not scheduled a miracle for that day, but a few well-said words by a loving mother rearranged those plans. Suddenly Jesus performed his first miracle at the insistence of his mother (John 2:1-11).

One verse of Scripture serves as a lens for understanding Mary's special relationship with her firstborn: "But Mary treasured up all these things and pondered them in her heart" (Luke 2:19). These words appear in the middle of the story about the shepherds coming to worship the newborn child. So many things had already happened that Mary didn't understand or that amazed her. So she began tucking these thoughts away in the back of her mind and reflecting on them later. No doubt, she did this frequently throughout Jesus' lifetime.

All of these pondered thoughts perhaps came to her conscious mind and erupted in the form of uncontrollable cries and screams at the foot of Jesus' cross. "How can this be the Father's plan?" she cried. "How can this be happening to my son?" Jesus transferred responsibility of his mother to his disciple John in those final moments on the cross. The passage seems to indicate that John quoted Mary as she related the actual words Jesus spoke to her (John 19:25-27).

This book focuses on the lordship of Jesus Christ. Mary gave birth to Jesus. She raised him from infancy and invested her entire heart and life into his. She surrendered many of her personal ambitions to fulfill the Father's plan for her life. So how do we know she made Jesus Lord of her life? Because we find one short verse in the scriptural record that tells us so.

Following Jesus' crucifixion, all of his disciples (except Judas, who had already abandoned Jesus) ran for their lives and hid from the

Roman soldiers and Jewish religious leaders behind locked doors in secret locations. Many other followers lost faith in him. Following Jesus' resurrection, he appeared to his disciples in his resurrected body. He instructed them to wait for the Holy Spirit in Jerusalem.

The disciples gathered and began their wait following his ascension. It's safe to say that everyone who made the trip back to Jerusalem to wait on Jesus' promise was serious about maintaining allegiance to him as Lord. Some of those waiting together are named in Acts 1:13-14, and among them is "Mary the mother of Jesus" (v. 14). Yes, Mary could truly say, "Jesus is Lord!"

Mary serves as an important role model for us today.

John

As he was dying on the cross, Jesus entrusted the care of his mother to his disciple John (John 19:26-27). This action demonstrates to us the incredible confidence Jesus placed in John. Jesus selected John and his brother James to be his disciples early in his earthly ministry (Matt. 4:21). Their father, Zebedee, released them from their obligation in the family fishing business to travel with this new teacher. I believe he even gave them his blessing to enter the ministry with Jesus.

John grew up in Israel, received a normal Jewish religious education, and learned the fishing trade on the Sea of Galilee. But things changed dramatically for John once he joined Jesus' band of disciples. He listened to the teachings of Jesus and watched the example of Jesus. Overwhelming evidence convinced him that Jesus truly was the Messiah, for whom they had prayed and waited all these years.

Jesus took John into his innermost circle. We often read in Scripture of Jesus speaking or working with Peter, James, and John. For example, "He [Jesus] did not let anyone follow him except Peter, James and John the brother of James" (Mark 5:37). Before his transfiguration, "Jesus took with him Peter, James and John the brother of James, and led them up a high mountain by themselves" (Matt. 17:1).

John and his brother had the nickname "sons of thunder" (Mark 3:17) probably because of their dispositions to react quickly to whatever was happening. Examples of this include their immediate desire to call fire down and destroy a group of Samaritans when they resisted Jesus' message (Luke 9:51-56), their impulsive request to sit in places of honor in Jesus' coming kingdom (Mark 10:37), and their haste to reprimand disciples who were not in their particular group (Mark 9:38).

You notice that most of these Scripture references to John occur in the first three gospels. John wrote his own gospel account, the fourth gospel. Something changed in John's heart and life between the "sons of thunder" events and the time he wrote his gospel account. In the gospel of John, he was very humble and never referred to himself by name. He chose to stay in the background, only calling himself the "beloved disciple." It's as if he took John the Baptist's words about Jesus to heart, "He must become greater; I must become less" (John 3:30).

What do you suppose changed this man so radically from the time he first met Jesus until he wrote his gospel late in his life? So much happened right at the end of Jesus' earthly ministry. He witnessed Jesus' agony in the garden of Gethsemane. Along with Peter and James, he was in closest proximity to Jesus that last night when Jesus prayed his heartfelt prayer to his Father. He and Peter fled the scene when the soldiers arrived to arrest Jesus, and they followed Jesus at a distance to see what the soldiers did with him (18:15-16). In other words, he and Peter were cowards, because they denied their Lord in his hour of need.

Yet something in John changed on the morning of Jesus' resurrection (20:2). Notice how John referred to himself as the "other disciple, the one Jesus loved." That was John's way of staying out of the story to keep the attention on Jesus. This was Jesus' resurrection, and John didn't feel worthy to even name himself in the events of that day.

Perhaps the sight of the empty tomb, the postresurrection appearances of Jesus (20:19–21:23), and the coming of the Holy Spirit at

Pentecost (Acts 2) all answer our question of what changed John so radically. John believed the truths of Jesus' teaching from the early days of his ministry. But not until John made Jesus Lord of his entire life at Pentecost did John experience the thorough and profound transformation we witness later in his life.

John's story did not end with the gospel account, however. Early church tradition tells us that John was the only one of the eleven disciples of Jesus (twelve minus Judas Iscariot) who was not persecuted to death, though he did suffer persecution. We read in Rev. 1 of his persecution and banishment to the jail caves on the island of Patmos, where he wrote the book of Revelation. God's angel gave him the vision that he wrote in this book while serving his prison term on Patmos.

The Roman government eventually released John from prison. We are told he moved back to Ephesus, where he died of natural causes around AD 98. He became the early church's living historian and told stories about Jesus until his dying day. He wanted people to believe in Jesus (John 3:16) and "love one another" (13:35). Those were his two major themes in life.

John serves as an important role model for us today. We must make Jesus Lord of all and serve him fully every day of our lives, regardless of life's circumstances.

Stephen

John's long life of ministry for Jesus is sharply contrasted with Stephen's short life of ministry. Yet Stephen, too, illustrates an important example of making Jesus Lord of life. We read about Stephen and his ministry in Acts 6–7. What a glowing account it is! The original disciples of Jesus realized they needed assistants to help them as the early church grew rapidly. So they selected seven additional men to support them (6:3).

Stephen topped their list of choices. He must have been an outstanding spiritual leader in the early church. The Bible tells us he was wise (v. 3), "full of faith and of the Holy Spirit" (v. 5), as well as dedicated and set apart for Christian service (v. 6). Opposition to the Christian faith quickly arose from the Jewish religious leaders. Stephen stood his ground and responded to them instead of choosing to remain silent. His arguments were filled with wisdom and the Holy Spirit (v. 10). The religious leaders reacted to Stephen the same way they had to Jesus: they found false witnesses to bring false charges against him.

Acts 7 in many translations of the Bible begins with the title "Stephen's Speech to the Sanhedrin." That is an accurate heading. However, there are some additional things to keep in mind. On the lighter side, Stephen's speech is the longest speech in the book of Acts. It also occupies an important place in the book, because its message is the central message of the book of Acts.

More importantly, Stephen's speech is the early church's first apology or defense of the gospel message. It explained in full detail the entire Old Testament story of how God's plan of salvation for humanity included Gentiles as well as Jews. Its message offered eternal hope for all peoples of the world. Unfortunately, the Jews weren't so inclusive in wanting to offer their salvation to outsiders. They had one word for Stephen's speech—"blasphemy."

Notice from the speech that Stephen did not back down as he brought the Old Testament story to the time of Jesus' arrival on earth. He laid full blame for the crucifixion of Jesus on the Jewish Sanhedrin, the religious ruling body of the people to whom he spoke (vv. 51-54). Notice, too, that the Holy Spirit inspired him to speak this message and empowered his words as he spoke them. The Holy Spirit literally filled him to enable him to represent Jesus Christ in this manner to the religious authorities (v. 55).

Being the wise man that he was, Stephen knew how that day would likely end for him. But that was all right with him. He began the day with his mind made up. He had settled the matter long ago. Jesus was his Lord, and no religious ruling body was going to intimidate him to dilute the message of the gospel. He would declare it with resolve and pay the consequences with his life, if need be. And so, Stephen's speech ended with Stephen becoming the first martyr for the Christian faith.

Did you get that? His witness to his faith led to his martyrdom for his faith. Strange disconnect, you say? No! Not at all! You see, in Greek—the original language of the New Testament—"to witness" and "to martyr" come from the same family of words. So "to bear witness" can also mean "to give one's life as a martyr." That does not mean one must follow the other. However, the first meaning does relate to the second one. So early Christians knew what they were getting themselves into. If they witnessed to their allegiance to Jesus Christ, they might be signing their own death warrant.

Stephen serves as important role model for us today. He reminds us that when we say "Jesus is Lord," we must say it with resolve and conviction. We must say it with the commitment that even if it costs us our lives, then so be it—we're willing to pay that price. Today, brothers and sisters in Christ are saying "Jesus is Lord" in some parts of our world and dying for it. Will you join them with a willing heart? That's all he asks—a willing heart.

Do you think Stephen's influence ended the day the stones of the Sanhedrin ended his earthly life? Absolutely not! The Scripture says that Stephen "fell asleep" (v. 60) and the Lord Jesus took him home. But a young man was standing in the crowd, taking in the whole scene and liking what he saw (8:1). That is, until the Lord got a hold of his heart—and then trouble for the Sanhedrin was just getting started.

Paul

Paul, named Saul at birth, was born in Tarsus, capital of Cilicia, a Roman province in Asia Minor. Tarsus was a wealthy city with sizable commercial traffic and a major university. So Paul enjoyed the benefits of a highly developed civilization and a first-rate education. He had a pure Jewish lineage, and his father was a Pharisee from the tribe of Benjamin (Phil. 3:5). He knew Jewish law well and followed it carefully. Using his own words, he said about himself, "As for righteousness based on the law, [I am] faultless" (v. 6).

Paul's father enjoyed the benefit and privilege of Roman citizenship. Scripture does not tell us if he bought it or received it for distinguished service to the state. Nevertheless, he was able to bestow this privilege on Paul. As Paul began his teen years, his family decided he should become a Jewish rabbi. So he studied the elaborate details of Jewish religious law and Scripture in preparation for his profession. He studied many years in Jerusalem under the famous rabbi Gamaliel. He then returned to his hometown and learned a trade—tent making, a common skill in Tarsus.

Paul probably then returned to Jerusalem about the time of Christ's crucifixion. He heard Stephen's eloquent speech before the Sanhedrin that we discussed above. His strict Jewish training caused him to hear only blasphemy in Stephen's words. So he agreed with the verdict of the Sanhedrin to stone Stephen to death. He also agreed with the plot of the Jewish leaders to rid Christianity from the land. He even participated in this plan, traveling from town to town to persecute Christians.

Then something went terribly wrong with his persecution plans. You can read the whole story in its various forms in Acts 9, 22, and 26. The Lord Jesus Christ himself appeared to Paul on the road to Damascus and stopped him dead in his tracks. Talk about a radical transformation! No wonder Paul wrote so eloquently in his thirteen New Testament letters about the life-changing power of the gospel. He was living proof of it.

We said at the beginning of this book that Paul loved to talk about the lordship of Christ. His letters explode with the thought. Jesus became Paul's Lord on the Damascus Road. Paul went from persecuting Christians to promoting Christ in this one transforming moment. Everything about his life changed the hour Jesus became his Lord. Then he spent the rest of his life taking the gospel message to the Gentiles. He became the Sanhedrin's worst nightmare. Everything about him testified for Jesus, as he went about living, preaching, writing, suffering, and finally dying for his Lord.

Paul serves as an important role model for us today. He grew up in religious tradition and knew the Bible well, but he didn't have a personal relationship with Jesus Christ. He thought he had all the answers through a good education but found he had much to learn. The important thing is, when he encountered Christ in a real way, he admitted his need, confessed his sin, and let God have his way with his life. He truly made Jesus his Lord and then spent the rest of his life helping others come to know his Lord as well.

Conclusion

The New Testament contains much information and many examples of the lordship of Christ. This chapter barely scratches the surface. Hopefully, something you have read in this chapter will pique your interest to dig deeper and study more for yourself.

The life and ministry of Jesus offers many examples and lessons on the lordship of Christ. The history of the Christian church and its expansion, as recorded in the book of Acts, recounts the seriousness with which Jesus' disciples took his lordship, as they declared the gospel message everywhere they went. Stephen's story is just one of many disciples' stories in that rich tradition. The letters from Peter, John, and Paul remind us that men and women in churches near and far enjoyed new life in Christ and lived lives daily under the lordship of Christ.

The New Testament is a rich resource recounting the earliest days of the Christian church. It was from that long-ago time that we received the wonderful declaration, "Jesus is Lord!"

THINK ABOUT THIS

1. Why did the resurrection of Jesus have such a powerful impact on his disciples in helping them realize that he was truly the Messiah?

2. Why was it so important for the early Christian church to move worship from the last day of the week to the first day of the week?

3. What are some of the things Mary treasured up and pondered in her heart about Jesus?

4. What important lesson do you learn from the example of Mary?

5. What important lesson do you learn from the example of John?

6. What important lesson do you learn from the example of Stephen?

7. Why do you think God chose Paul to take the gospel message to the Gentiles?

8. What important lesson do you learn from the example of Paul?

PRACTICE THIS

1. Copy the Phil. 2:5-11 passage onto a notecard and say it several times a day for a week. At the end of the week, see if you can recite the passage from memory. Now list the ways this attitude of Jesus can make a difference in the way you live your daily life. Place that list in a prominent place where you can see it every day, and let it form your behavior.

2. Select one of the four Bible personalities presented in this chapter (Mary, John, Stephen, or Paul). List five ways in which this person is a role model for you. Now list action steps you can take to become more like that person and in so doing reflect Jesus as Lord.

CHAPTER

THE BEST-KEPT
SECRET—REVEALED

He [God] made known to us

the mystery of his will according

to his good pleasure, which he

purposed in Christ, to be put into

effect when the times reach their

fulfillment—to bring unity to all

things in heaven and on earth

under Christ.

—Eph. 1:9-10

"Don't accept candy from strangers." Every child probably hears that warning a hundred times. It reminds children that they need to be careful whom they trust. Some people might not be worthy of their trust. A national television reporter recently conducted a secret experiment with children. A stranger drove an ice-cream truck to a park and invited children to get in the truck to select their favorite flavor of ice cream. All three children playing nearby climbed into the truck with the man. Because it was a televised experiment, the children were safe, but they failed the experiment by trusting the stranger. We must teach our children to be careful whom they trust.

The same principle applies to adults. Take investments, for instance. We need to know whom we can trust with our retirement funds. Financial advisors line up at our door to offer their services and charge a fee to get their hands on our hard-earned money. We cannot trust all of them.

It will be a long time before anyone rivals the financial mismanagement accomplished by Bernie Madoff. Perhaps, no one will ever match what he did. Madoff tricked investors into giving him $60 billion to invest for them—or more accurately, to put in his own personal bank account so he could spend it on his lavish lifestyle. He brought financial ruin to hundreds of individuals and several high-profile nonprofit organizations. So we need to be careful whom we trust.

This warning holds especially true for the one to whom you decide to give your life's allegiance. Who are you going to call Lord? You have an almost endless list of prospective lords calling for your attention and allegiance. You will make a choice, either consciously or unconsciously. That's why it's important for you to consider the credentials of Jesus Christ. As you do so, you will discover why he is truly worthy of your allegiance. In this chapter we will explore the areas over which he exerts his influence in our world.

Jesus Is Lord over All Creation
and Its Preservation

Several years ago, an advertising campaign began displaying on billboards and city busses in the United States and Western Europe ads denying the existence of God. Sponsored by a new brand of atheism, the campaign brandished such slogans as, "In the Beginning, Man Created God" and "There's probably no God. Now stop worrying and enjoy your life."[1] Richard Dawkins expressed similar thoughts in his 2008 book *The God Delusion*. Dawkins, perhaps the world's most well-known atheist, argues that belief in God is not only intellectually wrong but also dangerous for human advancement.

Denying God's existence is an amazing feat. It takes an enormous amount of faith to doubt that an intelligent Being created the world. Norman Geisler, Frank Turek, and David Limbaugh offer a similar idea in their book *I Don't Have Enough Faith to Be an Atheist*. They maintain that denying the existence of God requires more blind faith than it does to believe in Jesus Christ. When you press the most intellectual of atheists about where and how they think our world began, they admit they have no idea.

Atheists, in general, build their beliefs on questionable foundations, believing, for the most part, what they choose to believe. When an atheist was asked on a recent radio talk show how he could continue to deny God in the midst of such a wonderful created order, he replied, "I choose not to think about such things."[2]

Christians, unlike atheists, believe firmly that Jesus involved himself fully in the creation of all reality and that he actively participates daily in the preservation of that reality. Let's explore these two ideas further.

The Bible nowhere tries to prove the existence of God; it simply takes his existence for granted. Genesis 1:1 begins with God already on the scene before he brought the world into existence. We humans have birthdays, and so do all created things—the earth, other planets, galaxies, and so on. The triune God, however, does not have a birthday. Think of it, there never was a time when God was not. He even "predates" time itself! As Paul put it in Col. 1:17, "He is before all things."

This One who created all things identified himself to Moses in Exod. 3:14 as "I AM WHO I AM." The Great I Am is the Source of all beings and all "beingness." He is the God of Noah, Abraham, Isaac, Jacob, and Joseph.

Several passages of Scripture analyze Christ's involvement in the creation of the world. One significant example is Col. 1:15-20:

> The Son is the image of the invisible God, the firstborn over all creation. For in him all things were created: things in heaven and on earth, visible and invisible, whether thrones or powers or rulers or authorities; all things have been created through him and for him. He is before all things, and in him all things hold together. And he is the head of the body, the church; he is the beginning and the firstborn from among the dead, so that in everything he might have the supremacy. For God was pleased to have all his fullness dwell in him, and through him to reconcile to himself all things, whether things on earth or things in heaven, by making peace through his blood, shed on the cross.

Many scholars believe the thought for this passage comes from an early Christian hymn that contained the collective thought of the early church on the supremacy of Christ. Christians wanted to affirm his lordship from the earliest days of church history.

We notice first in this passage that Christ gives us a perfect picture of our invisible God.[3] Next, we see that the Father chose to create the world and everything in it through the Son. As we just observed, Christ existed before all creation, so he was never created as we were. We next notice that Christ is Lord over the church, victor over death, and superior to everything we know now or will ever know. All of the power, knowledge, and ability of the Father dwell fully in the Son. Most importantly for us, Christ opened the way for us to have peace with God through his shed blood on the cross.

Without a doubt, Jesus Christ is Lord over all creation—first, because he created it and, second, because he redeemed it. But that's not all. Not only is he Lord over all creation, but he also carefully preserves it daily, with loving care.

As creation's preserving Lord, Jesus is sort of like white glue. Remember white glue? Most of us have probably used white glue for craft projects at school. We mainly used the stuff to hold together our construction-paper and Popsicle-stick projects. When we looked at our finished creations, we credited the trusty white glue with holding it all together. We didn't think much about it, because when it dries, white glue turns clear and disappears. We didn't see it, but it was still present doing its job of holding things together.

Do you ever think about what holds the molecules together that make up matter in our world? Scientists don't know. After all of their research, tests, and calculations, they end up with inadequate explanations and simply have to admit that they can't explain what holds everything together.

Again, from the days of the New Testament, the church has long known the answer. Christ the Creator is also the Preserver of his creation. He's the glue that holds it all together. Augustine of Hippo (AD 354–430) once said that if God removed his hand from our world, even for a moment, it would immediately disintegrate.

Jesus demonstrated his lordship over his creation when he calmed the storm on the lake, as recounted in Mark 4:35-41. His disciples reacted with both awe and wonder about who he was. As we read in Luke 8:25, "Who is this? He commands even the winds and the water, and they obey him." The Old Testament made it clear that God rules over the waves of the sea (Ps. 89:9). In calming the storm, Jesus demonstrated power known only to God. Jesus is truly Lord of all creation.[4]

Jesus Is Lord over the Nations and All Humanity

Things are not always as they appear. In the novel *Great Expectations*, by Charles Dickens, the story's main character, Pip, seemed to prosper with his every endeavor. It's almost as if someone was going before him preparing the way—and someone indeed was doing just that. Abel Magwitch, an escaped convict, dedicated his life to working quietly behind the scenes to give Pip every advantage in life. On the surface, it looked as though Pip was doing quite well for himself. In reality, his benefactor watched in the shadows as he carried out his plan in the life of his young friend.

To some people, claiming that Christ is currently Lord of the nations of this world and all humanity may seem to be an odd observation. Political unrest plagues nearly every continent of the world. Dictators and totalitarian governments harshly rule millions of people. Refugees, trying to escape politically oppressive rulers, are herded into overcrowded camps with subhuman living conditions. Ethnic cleansings continue to make headlines in spite of promises by politically powerful nations to prevent such things. More and more nations are aiming nuclear warheads at one another. Wars rage globally.

It sounds hopeless, doesn't it? It sounds as if the leadership of the nations has fallen chaotically out of control, leaving millions of innocent citizens deprived of their basic human rights. It sounds like global pandemonium.

Things, however, are not always as they appear. Christ won a decisive victory against Satan, evil, and sin on the cross. He defeated death through his bodily resurrection. Those of us who have trusted in him as personal Savior have realized some of the immediate effects of that victory. We are new creatures in Christ (2 Cor. 5:17), and we have abundant life (John 10:10), with hope of an eternal future with him in heaven (Col. 1:5). That's just the beginning of this new venture with Christ.

When we make the seemingly odd observation that Christ is currently Lord of the nations of this world and all humanity, we do so through eyes of faith. We believe that what happened in the spiritual realm when Jesus died on the cross and rose from the dead will one day make an appearance in the physical realm for everyone on earth to see.

Peter captured this vision in his sermon on the day of Pentecost. "Therefore let all Israel be assured of this: God has made this Jesus, whom you crucified, both Lord and Messiah" (Acts 2:36). Through eyes of faith we believe that Jesus Christ holds the keys to the destiny of the nations and all humanity. Through eyes of faith we believe that the victory won through Christ's death and resurrection will one day bring to an end all forces that hold people in bondage and keep them from loving and serving the one and only God.

We are now in the waiting room. We live in between the "already" and the "not yet." Christ has already won the right to be Lord of the nations and all humanity, but he has not yet been enthroned in that position. His kingdom has begun and is present but still awaits its fulfillment. So we're caught in the disparity between the present reality and the future reality. What we see now is not the way it is always going to be. What we see now is not the way God wants things to be. Although we can't see Christ working quietly behind the scenes, in our hearts we know he is. Through eyes of faith we see that the future belongs to Christ.

Paul looked into this promising future. After making the observation that Christ won the victory over death through his resurrection, this is what he had to say about Christ ultimately bringing the nations under his control.

> Then the end will come, when he hands over the kingdom to God the Father after he has destroyed all dominion, authority and power. For he must reign until he has put all his enemies under his feet. The last enemy to be destroyed is death. For he "has put everything under his feet." Now when it says that "everything" has been put under him, it is clear that this does not

include God himself, who put everything under Christ. When he has done this, then the Son himself will be made subject to him who put everything under him, so that God may be all in all. (1 Cor. 15:24-28)

Even though this passage focuses on events occurring at the second coming of Christ, we find hints that even now Christ is working quietly behind the scenes to destroy the "dominion, authority and power" of the people and governments who oppose him. Even now! This doesn't happen overnight. It's a process that takes a long time. But nevertheless, Christ is even now working with the nations and all people to bring all things under his lordship. His kingdom is present and progressing to its fulfillment, when he will completely rule.

God has incredible patience for working through slow earthly processes. For instance, as we noted in chapter 3, there was the lengthy time it took for humanity to understand such a simple concept as the meaning of God's name. We want things to move quickly in our fast-paced world, but God is patient and willing to work at a slower pace. Always remember, in the end, God accomplishes his will. So we can take courage in Paul's vision of Christ working behind the scenes—even now.

John shared this same vision of Christ working quietly behind the scenes, even as world leaders refused to acknowledge Christ's lordship. See Rev. 11:15-19 for John's vision of things to come at the end of time. John wrote during a time of great persecution against Christians, who found themselves opposed by the Roman Empire, which clearly considered itself their political superior. The Romans exiled John to the island of Patmos to quiet his voice and limit his influence on the Christian movement.

But God didn't leave John to die alone on that island. He appeared to John and gave him visions of what was in store for the politically unstable world in which he lived. In the short run, Christians and their Christ appeared to have been neutralized by the powerful Roman Empire. But in the long run, the Roman Empire would implode—as will all governments that oppose God.

The cause of Christ, in contrast, has continued to this day to spread its influence to all of the nations of the world. Christ's kingdom survived the Roman Empire and every other empire that has opposed it down through the ages. Government leaders have tried their best to rid the world of Christianity. All have failed. Their efforts have done nothing but fan the flames of growth for Christ's cause.

Without getting into interpretations of all of the rich and complex imagery of John's visions while on the island of Patmos, suffice it to say that John's message carried a simple truth: God's will ultimately triumphs in the end! He will reign supreme as Lord of all other lords.

So if God is God—and he is—then he now exercises more control over the current global community than we may realize. This remains true even though many of earth's citizens do not acknowledge Christ as Lord. In ways broader than our minds can comprehend, even now Christ has ultimate control of the nations and all humanity.

God ordained civil government and approves of government providing basic services for its citizens, securing peace, and leading people wisely. God sets the bounds within which human governments can operate. When poor leaders violate those bounds, he limits their efforts and gives their rule to others. This concept is discussed by Paul in Rom. 13:1-7 and echoed in Jer. 27:5 and Ps. 75:7, where the psalmist says of God, "He brings one down, he exalts another."

Often this idea does not seem to reflect reality—especially if we watch the evening news. Paul understood this seeming inconsistency and in Eph. 1:10 reminded us that someday things will match up as they should when Christ brings his entire plan together. On that day, Christ will complete the process of uniting the nations and all humanity under his lordship. He will hand the entire completed work to his Father, who will then assume the role of administrative head for all eternity (see 1 Cor. 15:24-28).[5] When that happens, salvation history for humanity will be complete, and all who are citizens of God's kingdom will enjoy his leadership forever.

Now, that's a big plan, and it has millions of moving pieces. But Christ will someday bring all of those pieces together into a beautiful picture.

Jesus Is Lord over All Religion

We can't talk about the nations and all humanity without saying a word about the world's religions. The vast plurality of cultures, philosophies, customs, languages, histories, and peoples of the world brings with it a plurality of religious thinking as well. What do Christians say about the religions of the world in the light of the claim that Jesus is Lord?

That frequently asked question finds its way into everyday conversations these days on every continent of our globe. More than at any time in the history of humanity, the religions of the world are bumping into one another. People of different faiths have to find ways to coexist in peace. Yet their differences remain. How do we interpret the validity of these faiths? What do we say about their claims of giving their adherents spiritual fulfillment?

Peter Toon, in his book *Jesus Christ Is Lord*, discussed this matter in a chapter titled "Jesus, Lord of All Religions." Toon acknowledged that other religions of the world call their spiritual guides "lord." Krishna is lord of the Hindus, while Buddha is lord of the Buddhists. Toon presented four approaches commonly advocated for comparing the religions of the world. Comparative religion discussions basically fall into one of these four categories.

1. We can find salvation through all of the religions of the world. Each and every world religion developed over time within a particular culture. Therefore, in our pluralistic world with its infinite variety, no one religion can claim superior status as Christianity does. We must conclude for all of them, "To each his own."

2. All religions point followers to the same God. Those who believe this position say worshippers simply call upon God by different names due to their ethnic, geographic, climatic, linguistic, and historical conditioning.

3. God is the Lord of history and has a plan for the salvation of all humanity; this plan articulates differently in the various religions of the world. It's as if God scattered divine truth about himself and human salvation like seed throughout all of the religions of the world. The seed sprouted within each religion and developed uniquely based on cultural differences. All religions of the world hold divine truth; they simply express it differently. Leaders from all of the world religions should sit together and put their understandings of God on the table. All of these puzzle pieces will assemble to form a more complete picture. Only then can we find God's revelation. We must humbly learn from one another.

4. All religion by its very definition fails to meet the longing of human hearts. Religion is usually defined as humanity's search for God. We reach up with our hearts and minds to try to imagine who God is and what he expects from true worshippers. Religion is a human effort to reach up through prayer and devotion and bring God down to our understanding. We pray, offer various forms of worship, and do good toward others. But no human effort can adequately apprehend a proper understanding of God. So all religions of the world fall short.

Christianity, on the other hand, is not technically a religion. It is not humanity reaching up; rather, it is God reaching down to give us a revelation of himself through the incarnation, ministry, death, and resurrection of Jesus Christ. We didn't figure God out; he told us about himself and how to find salvation through Christ. Justification by grace through faith celebrates not what we do to find God but what God did to find us in Christ.[6]

In the parable of the lost sheep, as told by Jesus in Luke 15:3-7, the little sheep did not get on a computer and find a map to search its way back to the sheepfold. Rather, the shepherd ventured out, searched for, and brought back the sheep. All effort came from the shepherd. Jesus told that story to give us a crystal clear picture of God searching for lost humanity and bringing us back. That picture is the essence of the Christian faith. That picture is what makes Christianity different from the other religions of the world. We do not reach up to God; he reaches down to us.

So in every sense of the word, we can say Jesus Christ is Lord over all religion. We do not make this claim because "We're Christians, and we're number one!" We make this claim because we are recipients of the free gift of God's revelation of himself through Jesus Christ. Notice the focus shifts away from finding a superior religion to finding God's presentation of himself.

Take a look at a few unique features of the Christian faith:

- Jesus came to earth as a flesh-and-blood person; unlike many religious figures of other faiths, he was not a mythological figure.

- Only Jesus claimed to be preexistent with the Father prior to the creation of the world.

- Only Jesus lived a life of perfect righteousness and offered his life on the cross for the forgiveness of human sin, thus making salvation not what religious acts we do but what God did for us.

- Only Jesus rose from the dead. All other spiritual leaders died, were buried, and remained dead.

- Only faith in Jesus Christ meets the deep spiritual needs of human hearts of all cultures in the world. New life in Christ brings joy and peace with God and an end to spiritual searching.

- Only faith in Jesus Christ establishes a daily relationship with God and offers communication on a two-way street between Creator and creature.[7] The religions of the world do not offer their followers a warm, personal relationship with their gods.[8]

You may find it helpful to remember that this is not the first time in human history when cultural relativism gave humanity a variety of lords from which to choose. Both the Old and New Testaments offer numerous examples of religious pluralism. That's why Old Testament believers (Deut. 10:17; Ps. 136:3), as well as New Testament followers (1 Tim. 6:15; Rev. 17:14), called our God "Lord of lords." People have many lords calling for their allegiance. Jesus remains Lord over all of them. As Paul put it in 1 Cor. 8:4-6, "'There is no God but one.' For even if there are so-called gods, whether in heaven or on earth (as indeed there are many 'gods' and many 'lords'), yet for us there is but one God, the Father, from whom all things came and for whom we live; and there is but one Lord, Jesus Christ, through whom all things came and through whom we live."

Jesus Is Lord over the Church

Almost all of us have watched the construction of a new store belonging to a national chain that already seems to have a store at every corner of town. A chain of stores like this is committed to having a branch location in every neighborhood. Moreover, executives for such a company often have a master plan for providing their service to every neighborhood in the state.

Though we may not think about it in the same way, Jesus Christ has a similar master plan. He wants a branch location of his body (the body of Christ) in every community in the world. He wants to make his presence available to as many people as possible. He would like a community of faith within walking distance or a short drive for every person on this earth.

Paul developed this idea about the body of Christ in at least a half dozen places in his letters. In 1 Cor. 12, Paul offered an extended explanation of the way the church functions as Christ's hands and feet on the earth. He strongly emphasized the importance of all believers working together for this common goal. In verse 27 he said, "Now you are the body of Christ, and each one of you is a part of it." He offered similar instruction in Rom. 12:4-8 and Eph. 4:11-16. Take the time to read each of these passages of Scripture; they are worth the effort because they will add insight into Paul's thought on this subject.

In keeping with Christ's vision for the church as his body on the earth, Paul also expressed his desire that every local congregation be filled with believers who live lives that give people a flesh-and-blood picture of God at work in his world. He wanted individuals to be filled with and controlled by the Holy Spirit and to use the gifts and graces given by the Spirit to build up the church and witness to the world. He wanted fruit to spring from their lives that would stand as evidence that God lived within them, and their harmony with one another to show how God's love manifests itself within believers. In brief, he wanted each local faith congregation to serve as a microcosm of the total body of Christ, both on earth and in heaven. What an ingenious plan!

One fact remains unchallenged about the body of Christ—Jesus Christ is always its one and only head. Paul made that perfectly clear in Eph. 1:22; 4:15; 5:23, as well as Col. 1:18; 2:19. As head of the body of Christ, then, Christ must be Lord of the church and each believer who belongs to it. The Father has declared it should be this way. We're reminded in Eph. 1:22-23, "And God placed all things under his feet and appointed him to be head over everything for the church, which is his body, the fullness of him who fills everything in every way."

Jesus Is Lord over Time and Eternity

We stated in the last chapter that when Jesus visited earth, he preached and taught about the Father and invited us into a relationship with him. The ultimate validation for his life and ministry came when the Father raised him from the dead. The resurrection of Jesus Christ, more than any other event in human history, proved that Jesus is Lord.

Like his resurrection, Christ's ascension into heaven gave early Christians further proof of his lordship. They described Christ's ascension in two segments: (1) his liftoff from the earth (Acts 1:9) and (2) his return to a seat at the right hand of the Father in heaven (Mark 16:19). Let's take a closer look at these two events.

The liftoff of Jesus from the earth marked the moment when he left our world. It's the only world we have ever known, but for Jesus it signaled a return to his original home with the Father and Holy Spirit.

When we imagine this event in our mind's eye, we often compare it to a space shuttle blasting off from Cape Canaveral, Florida. Like a space shuttle, Jesus' resurrected body began to rise above the earth. However, this analogy breaks down quickly. A space shuttle would travel several miles above the earth's surface and begin circling the earth as it settled into a cruising altitude for the duration of its mission. Then it would return to the earth's surface. It never escaped the watchful eye of surveillance satellites; it never left our dimension of reality.

Jesus, on the other hand, left not only earth's surface but also earth's dimension of reality. Somewhere along his journey that day, he crossed over into the realm of eternity. Probably he did not have to travel millions of light-years; he simply crossed over into this other dimension we know as heaven. His successful journey that day reminds us that he is Lord over the path between earth's reality and eternity's. Thinking about his journey that day is exciting, because he blazed a trail for us. Someday we'll get to join him and all of our Christian loved ones who have preceded us.

Early followers of Christ often visualized Jesus' reception into his heavenly home by reading one of the psalms of ascent. Old Testament pilgrims sang these psalms of ascent as they walked together along the path to Jerusalem preparing their hearts to celebrate a major festival at the temple. Early Christians selected Ps. 24 as a fitting reminder of Jesus' return to his Father. Take a moment and read Ps. 24 right now. Like the early church, imagine Jesus being received into his heavenly home, having triumphed over sin, evil, and death. Visualize him entering as the great Conqueror while the hosts of heaven recite Ps. 24. He indeed is the King of glory!

Along with transitioning from the earthly realm back to the heavenly eternal realm, Jesus also reassumed his place, seated at the right hand of his Father. This event has multiple references in the New Testament; they are all important. Take a moment and read them: Mark 14:62; Eph. 1:20-21; Col. 3:1; Heb. 1:3; 8:1; 12:2; and 1 Pet. 3:22.

Mark 14:62 finds Jesus on trial before the high priest. Jesus' response to the high priest refers to Ps. 110:1 (also Dan. 7:13). The Hebrew people interpreted this as a prophetic reference to the coming of the Messiah; Jesus applied the words to himself. He made a similar reference earlier in the week while teaching in the temple courts. See Mark 12:35-37; Matt. 22:41-46; and Luke 20:41-44 for the context of his words. Jesus clearly applied Ps. 110 to his ascension back to the Father and his rule over all things.

Paul envisioned this same picture of Jesus sitting at the right hand of the Father in Eph. 1:19-21: "That power is the same as the mighty strength he [God] exerted when he raised Christ from the dead and seated him at his right hand in the heavenly realms, far above all rule and authority, power and dominion, and every name that is invoked, not only in the present age but also in the one to come." Paul clearly intended to present Jesus as Lord over all things: rulers, authorities, powers, dominions, titles, this age, and the one to come. All things are under his feet; he rules as head over everything. No one rivals Jesus. No one even comes close. He alone receives the highest honor the Father can bestow on any being in all of reality.

The book of Hebrews also echoed Ps. 110:1 in Heb. 1:3; 8:1; 12:2. The entire book attempted to establish that Jesus Christ, as Deity, is superior to everything known in religious tradition. The climax of this argument placed Christ superior to earthly high priests. Our High Priest, Jesus Christ, occupies a special seat in heaven.

Again, this throne imagery reminds us of Christ's superior position in heaven. Jesus occupies not just any heavenly seat but the best seat in the house. His placement at the right hand of the Father makes him second in command, according to our human understanding.

For us, this means Jesus has all power and authority over everything in both heaven and earth. He remains the only One ever named as having this special place next to his Father. This special placement tells us that he deserves our worship as our Lord.

Peter echoed the same sentiment in 1 Pet. 3:21-22 as Paul and the writer of Hebrews did. "It [water baptism] saves you by the resurrection of Jesus Christ, who has gone into heaven and is at God's right hand—with angels, authorities and powers in submission to him." He used the image of Jesus at the right hand of the Father to indicate Jesus' royal power and dignity. He wanted us to know that all angels, authorities, and powers in our universe, both good and evil, are subject to Christ's lordship.[9]

These passages taken together teach us that Christ is superior to all created beings in heaven and on earth. He not only represents the Father but is a perfect reflection of him. He triumphed over every enemy who stood to oppose him, and he will continue to do so until he vanquishes all his enemies. All his enemies will eventually take their rightful place under his feet. The Father has entrusted all power and authority to his Son, who will safely bring to his side all who trust in him; they will eventually triumph with him. That includes us!

Conclusion

The images found in these last several scriptures leave Jesus sitting at the right hand of the Father—waiting. Waiting for what? Waiting for a word from the Father that the time has arrived to lay claim to the victory secured by his death on the cross—a victory kept for final fulfillment at the end of time. That is when everything we have discussed in this chapter will reach completion, and the "not yet" will be today.

When all that happens, Christ's kingdom will be complete, his rule absolute; every being in the universe will bow before Jesus and declare him Lord of all: "That at the name of Jesus every knee should bow, in heaven and on earth and under the earth, and every tongue acknowledge that Jesus Christ is Lord, to the glory of God the Father" (Phil. 2:10-11).

But until then, Paul reminded us that the Lord Jesus Christ has ultimate control over all rule, authority, power, and dominion on this earth. When analyzed from the perspective of our daily lives, that pretty much covers every trial and temptation we will ever face from now until then! Christ is truly in control now, although at times it doesn't seem like it. Christ will win the final battle against good and evil at the end of time. He will win the victory once and for all. Everyone and everything will bow before him on that great day—because Jesus is Lord![10]

THINK ABOUT THIS

1. Why do you suppose the Bible does not attempt to prove the existence of God?

2. List some of the ways Christ preserves our world daily.

3. Give examples from history of God limiting the rule of harsh government leaders.

4. How does God's revealing himself to humanity through the incarnation of Jesus Christ make Christianity totally different from all of the religions of the world?

5. How does the image of Jesus sitting at the right hand of the Father in heaven help you in understanding his lordship?

6. In most of the areas discussed in this chapter, Christ balances his plan and control of events with human free will. Why does he take human free will so seriously as he works through these matters?

PRACTICE THIS

1. Imagine you are an atheist for a few minutes. Think of all of the leaps of faith you must make to deny God's existence.

2. Think of ways you and your small group can demonstrate to those outside the church that you are the hands and feet of Jesus as members of the body of Christ.

PART TWO

MAKING JESUS LORD OF OUR DAILY LIVES

Now the attention of this book turns to us. Up to this point, we have looked out in other directions. We first looked broadly across nearly two thousand years of Christian tradition to see how other believers have understood the affirmation that Jesus is Lord. Not only did early Christians declare this truth with their mouths and believe it in their hearts, but they also willingly laid down their lives before they would deny it.

Next we turned to the Bible for a scriptural understanding of lordship. We looked at the development of the concept throughout the Old Testament in the lives of some of God's special people. Then we turned our attention to the New Testament and saw the image of Lord fully developed in the person of Jesus Christ. Again, we viewed the concept through the lives of some of God's special people. They truly knew what it meant to live a life that testified, "Jesus is Lord!"

Now we fast-forward to the twenty-first century. What does all of that information mean for us today? How do we apply it so that our lives witness to our world that Jesus is Lord? Those are questions we want to answer as we continue our study.

CHAPTER SIX

RECYCLED LORDS

Do people make their own

gods? Yes, but they are

not gods!

—Jer. 16:20

Both the Old and New Testaments speak of our God competing in the hearts of people with other gods and other lords. Joshua confronted this problem directly with his people as they conquered the Promised Land. He plainly said, "But if serving the LORD seems undesirable to you, then choose for yourselves this day whom you will serve, whether the gods your ancestors served beyond the Euphrates, or the gods of the Amorites, in whose land you are living. But as for me and my household, we will serve the LORD" (Josh. 24:15).

This reminds us again that religious pluralism dates back to our earliest recorded history. Other gods during the Old Testament period included Baal, Asherah, Chemosh, Dagon, and Molech. Other gods during the New Testament period included Zeus, Isis, Adonis, Demeter, Caesar, and Diana. The lordship of Christ in the early church meant early Christians purposefully chose to identify themselves with Jesus Christ rather than one of the gods of other religions.

When we contemplate the meaning of Christ's lordship in the twenty-first century, we usually do not think of having to steer away from other world religions. Probably few, if any, of us have given serious consideration to worshipping Allah, practicing Buddhist meditations, or applying Hindu principles to daily living.

But we do hear the tempting voices of different kinds of gods. These voices usurp the lordship of Christ and sneak in among us in subtle ways. As you read the sections of this chapter, think about ways these lords call for your attention. Perhaps these particular voices may not call to you; other voices, just as subtle, just as tempting, however, do call your name. So be on guard. Remember the warning of the prophet Jeremiah: "Do people make their own gods? Yes, but they are not gods!" (Jer. 16:20).

Human Ingenuity

We are such clever creatures that we often impress ourselves. Without even trying, we can subtly remove Jesus Christ from the throne of lordship and put our combined abilities in his place. Think for a minute at our impressive accomplishments in science, technology, space travel, commercial airline travel, satellite navigation, communication, and entertainment. This list only scratches the surface of our many accomplishments. We have inventions of every sort to make life easier and more enjoyable, and without even trying, we find ourselves exalting human ingenuity.

The temptation to trust human ingenuity plagues every society. It begins when we are children, building things with sticks, string, and nails and then standing back to declare, "Look what I built!" That's the problem—the attitude behind that very declaration. Then we become self-sufficient. Human ingenuity easily slips into idolatry, subtly making it lord in our lives.

It's that attitude of the heart we find addressed in Gen. 11:1-4:

Now the whole world had one language and a common speech. As people moved eastward, they found a plain in Shinar and settled there. They said to each other, "Come, let's make bricks and bake them thoroughly." They used brick instead of stone, and tar for mortar. Then they said, "Come, let us build ourselves a city, with a tower that reaches to the heavens, so that we may make a name for ourselves; otherwise we will be scattered over the face of the whole earth."

Do you recognize the building project? The people were constructing the Tower of Babel. Does this passage of Scripture imply that God opposes all tall buildings? No, not at all. Otherwise, God would object to all large cities of our world. This passage focuses on the central question of this book: Who is lord of your life? The context of this passage implies that the builders began trusting their own human ingenuity more than they trusted God.

For us in the twenty-first century, does this mean scientific and technological advances are against God? No, it means we must guard our attitude toward them. Are we trusting in these advances more than we are trusting God? Ask yourself the following questions about the modern conveniences you enjoy from cell phones, iPads, and online shopping to Facebook, texting, and a thousand other recent developments. Answer these questions honestly and see how you view God in comparison to these devices and apps.

1. Do you control these things or do they control you?
2. Do you manage the amount of time you spend with them or do you spend all the time they require?
3. Do you manage the amount of money you spend with them or do you keep up with all the upgrades?
4. What place do these things have in the priorities of your day?
5. What place do these things have in your relationships with people?
6. Are these things just objects to you or do they have a special place in your life?

Constantly guard against allowing human ingenuity to become a lord in your life.

Human Recognition

Everyone appreciates being noticed by others. There's nothing wrong with that. God created our human nature to enjoy receiving recognition by others. We find it healthy to give and receive compliments.

It's one thing to appreciate recognition when it comes our way; it's quite another to live for it. Some people make it the goal of their lives. Here are a few ways this "lord" finds expression:

• We see it frequently when we watch the television news. A news reporter is standing on the street in front of a camera giving his or her report when pedestrians realize they are on camera too. What do they do? They look straight into the camera, wave, and say, "Hi, Mom!" Now, that is a trivial example, but like the examples that follow, it's an opportunity for individuals to get attention, to exclaim, "Look at me."

• Some people form their sentences in such a way that others feel obligated to pay them compliments. They put themselves down so others will tell them they are great. Or they say their work or their cooking is inferior so others will tell them their work is the best or their cooking is superior. They put people on the spot by asking, "So what do you think of my poem?" People then feel obligated to praise the poem's form and beauty, even if they have little idea what the poem means!

- Some people point out faults in others or gossip about them. They may not even realize why they feel the need to do it. Perhaps by bringing others down, they lift themselves up. In a job setting, they may want others to recognize them as having superior qualities that entitle them to a promotion or a pay raise.

- Some people when conversing socially feel the need to brag about their accomplishments to as many people as will listen to them. They talk about the educational degrees they have earned, the extensive travels they have enjoyed, the expensive cars they drive, the spacious homes they own, and so on. The list is almost endless—as are their conversations!

- Some people feel they have to win every game and contest in which they take part. Everyone must recognize them as the best—at everything. If they lose, they get upset. Often others prefer to let these people win than risk the consequences of their losing.

- Some students in school sit near the front of the class, perpetually poised to raise their hands and answer every question the teacher asks. Other students sit at the back of the room, disengaged, talking, and passing notes. Both types of students are seeking recognition in different ways.

All of these illustrations remind us of the countless approaches people take to seek human recognition. While there's nothing wrong with receiving a compliment when it's given, recognition can quickly take over a person's life and become a lord that demands more and more attention.

In chapter 4 we discussed how John's life radically changed after he made Jesus Lord of his life. Before John fully surrendered to the lordship of Jesus, this problem of human recognition plagued him. We read an example of it in Mark 10:35-45. John and his brother, James, made an important request of Jesus. "'What do you want me to do for you?' he asked. They replied, 'Let one of us sit at your right and the other at your left in your glory'" (vv. 36-37). The brothers wanted to be honored above all the other disciples in Jesus' coming kingdom.

Jesus taught an important spiritual truth about human recognition when he said, "You know that those who are regarded as rulers of the Gentiles lord it over them, and their high officials exercise authority over them. Not so with you. Instead, whoever wants to become great among you must be your servant, and whoever wants to be first must be slave of all. For even the Son of Man did not come to be served, but to serve, and to give his life as a ransom for many" (vv. 42-45).

We must constantly guard against allowing the need for human recognition to become a lord in our lives.

Money

Money, in and of itself, is not a problem. The monster rears its ugly head in what money does to people. It can destroy not only individual lives but also entire families. It can turn children against their parents, husbands against wives, and employees against their bosses and generally blur the meaning of life on earth.

The lordship problem with money isn't just in possessing it but also in wanting to possess it. There are people with almost no money who have made it their lord. They buy lottery tickets each week, hoping they will get a lucky break and win the millions of dollars they covet daily (and, in fact, worship). Many people spend countless hours worrying about their lack of money or wishing they had more of it. They are obsessed with money and what they believe it will do for them.

In the study of secular history, church history, politics, and religion, the expression "Follow the money trail" is often used to explain a chain of events or a series of decisions. Clearly, money down through the ages and across every culture of the world has served as a universal lord of the human heart.

Do you know why in the United States we call our currency the almighty dollar? Because many people serve it as lord. "Almighty" is a divine attribute. The term subtly reminds us of its power to gather worshippers. That's why people will do so many bad things to get it. The list is endless of the lengths people will go to get their hands on one more dollar bill. Bank or convenience store robberies make the news daily. Often the robbers take only a few dollars. Pickpockets and purse snatchers create problems for honest people worldwide.

Often people misquote Paul, saying, "Money is the root of all evil." They are thinking of 1 Tim. 6:10, where Paul said, "For the love of money is a root of all kinds of evil. Some people, eager for money, have wandered from the faith and pierced themselves with many griefs." It's not money itself that poses the problem; it's the love of money that gets us in trouble.

Remember our discussion of Abraham in chapter 3? Every indication of Scripture leads us to believe that in the culture of his day, Abraham was wealthy. He owned possessions, but his possessions did not own him. He knew their proper place in life. And more importantly, he kept God Lord of his life. That is the essential lesson for us!

In contrast to Abraham was the rich young man of Matt. 19:16-26. Jesus discussed money and the things that money can buy with this young man. We find the thrust of Jesus' message to this young man, however, not in what he said to the young man, but in what he did not say to him. The young man knew the Ten Commandments well. Notice that as Jesus recited the commandments having to do with the way people should treat others, he omitted one. The young man would have caught the omission immediately and thus heard Jesus' message to him without Jesus having to say another word. The omitted commandment was, "You shall not covet . . ." (Exod. 20:17). The young man not only had many possessions but also coveted even more possessions and the money needed to get them. Money had become his lord.

That's why Jesus said, "It is easier for a camel to go through the eye of a needle than for someone who is rich to enter the kingdom of God" (Matt. 19:24). His words directly relate to a message he gave earlier: "No one can serve two masters. Either you will hate the one and love the other, or you will be devoted to the one and despise the other. You cannot serve both God and money" (6:24).

Ask yourself the following questions about the role of money in your life.

- What is my relationship to my money?
- Do I own money or does it own me?
- Do I subtly serve money as almighty?
- What am I willing to sacrifice to have more money?

We must constantly guard against allowing the love of money to become a lord in our lives.

Personal Reputation

Our personal reputation has many features of human recognition about it. That is, God created our human nature to pursue the development of a good reputation. We'd certainly prefer having a good one than a bad one. Like human recognition, a good reputation takes time to develop.

Personal reputation concerns the way others view us. It has to do with our good or not-so-good name. It is formed by the sum total of our conduct, attitude, treatment of others, and demeanor across time. Although it takes a long time to develop a good reputation, a good reputation can be lost with one bad decision.

Sometimes people confuse personal reputation with character. Character represents the moral fiber that actually makes a person good. Personal reputation is the opinion others have about that person. This distinction becomes important when we begin to note the ways people allow themselves to bow at the shrine of reputation and make it their lord.

A Christian chorus, popular some time ago among teens, addressed this issue with the question, "What will people think?" The lyrics went on to ask what people would think if a person followed Christ and gave Christ his or her life. But the question gets at the heart of reputation. A reputation is formed by what people think about the way they see a person live his or her life.

Individuals aren't the only ones who cultivate reputations. Corporations build them as well. Many large corporations have reputation managers who work full time building and maintaining corporate credibility. Much of the advertising you see on television, on the Internet, in newspapers, and in magazines aims at building corporate reputations. Developing corporate reputations is a multibillion-dollar-a-year business.

In the light of all that, is it wrong for a Christian to seek a good reputation? Of course not! Every Christian should be a model citizen in every way. He or she should manifest the fruit of the Spirit (Gal. 5:22-23) and daily live a life in the Spirit of Christ (Rom. 8).

However, let's return to that question from the Christian chorus: "What would people think?"[1] What if that question plays in your head all day long? What if you live only to please others? What if all your decisions are based, not on what is good and right, but on how you look to the camera? That is a life of bondage. That is servitude to another god. That is making your personal reputation a lord.

Who lives like that? Think about it. In nearly every high-profile profession are servants bowing to this lord: Hollywood movie stars, television stars, sports stars, politicians, megachurch pastors, and so on. Wherever cameras and news reporters go, there you find people under pressure to worship the lord of personal reputation. Do only celebrities feel this pressure? No, ordinary people feel the pressure as well.

Several years ago, a movie came out about the life of Judy Garland. We remember her most for her role as Dorothy in the 1939 movie *The Wizard of Oz*, but she went on to star in other movies as well. She had a dysfunctional personal and family life. Her public relations manager was having a difficult time keeping her alcohol abuse and violent tantrums out of the newspaper. At one point in his frustration he asked, "Do you know how difficult it is to maintain the image of Judy Garland?" To which she screamed back at him, "Do you know how difficult it is to *be* Judy Garland?"[2]

The lord of personal reputation is a difficult lord to serve. "What would people think?" seems like such an innocent question. But that question can take complete control of your life if you're not careful. Scripture gives us a powerful admonition about this common problem through the life of a little-known man in a short book near end of the New Testament. In 3 John we read, "Demetrius is well spoken of by everyone—and even by the truth itself" (v. 12).

We know almost nothing about Demetrius's life other than that he carried John's letter to Gaius. But look what John said about his personal reputation. Everyone speaks well of him. More importantly, when his life is compared to the gospel of truth, it rings true. Now that's a testimony worth having! A person doesn't seek that reputation; it comes as a by-product of living the gospel message daily and letting Christ be Lord of his or her life.

We must constantly guard against allowing the need for personal reputation to become a lord in our lives.

Pleasure

Slogans from popular television commercials appeal to our innate desire for pleasure. Here are several we hear often:

"Just enjoy yourself."

"You work hard; you deserve a break."

"Of course it's expensive, but you're worth it."

"Do it for you."

Advertisers know you want to give yourself pleasure; they're betting billions of dollars that a few well-placed words at just the right time will be all the encouragement you need to go out, buy their product, and enjoy yourself.

So, is it wrong to enjoy yourself? Do the devil and his crowd get to have all of the fun? Does God expect us to sit around and work all of the time, avoiding pleasure at all cost? Of course not! However, like the previous topics we have considered, this one also has a legitimate and a not-so-legitimate fulfillment.

We often look to Jesus—the way he lived on earth, especially his interaction with his disciples—for clues to answer our questions. Jesus spent most of his last three years on earth with his disciples. Often they were in ministry settings, but they also spent time just sitting, relaxing, and talking about the events of the day. Jesus illustrated for us in those warm social settings the pleasure of human interaction. Not only did he impart information to his disciples, but he also truly seemed to enjoy his time together with them.

If Jesus illustrated a legitimate example of enjoying pleasure in life with his disciples, how can pleasure become a lord in our lives? When we live to run from one pleasure to another. Most developed nations have amusement parks. Families pay an entrance fee to enter the park. Once inside, family members can go on thrill rides, watch musical shows, shop, and eat in specialty restaurants all day. Young people generally run from one ride to another all day long and are exhausted when the day ends, as are their parents. But think of how many rides they enjoyed in a single day!

Sound crazy? Probably, but many people live their lives running from one pleasure to another. Some teenagers do this very thing. They take their cues from their school friends and live for pleasure. They can party away a weekend and then live all the next week for two more days of nonstop pleasure. Pleasure has become their highly revered lord, whom they serve wholeheartedly. The god of pleasure has their full devotion.

This behavior is not reserved to high school kids. Often it shifts into a higher gear once these kids reach adulthood. They work their jobs and care for their families, but as soon as they feel they are "off the clock," they bow to the lord of personal pleasure.

Just last week, a news reporter told of a famous television personality who hosts lavish parties on his multimillion-dollar yacht. The parties are around-the-clock events that last for days. The liquor flows freely; the food displays are updated hourly. No expense is spared as he and his guests serve the lord of pleasure together.

Although as Christians we do not stoop to these excesses, are there dangers we must guard against? Yes, indeed. It's not the amount of money spent on the pleasure that creates the problem. A homeless man living under the city bridge can be just as addicted to the pleasure he finds in cheap wine as the television star is to the pleasure he enjoys on his fancy yacht. They are both serving the lord of pleasure.

The problem is not the amount of money but the attitude of the heart toward the pleasure. It's the place the pleasure holds in our lives—the control it has over us—that's at issue. It's our need for more.

All of this assumes we are talking about pleasures that are consistent with our Christian witness. Ask yourself the following questions to be sure your pleasures are consistent with your witness:

- Is this consistent with the Bible?
- Is this good for me physically and mentally?
- Is this good for me spiritually?
- Is this consistent with my Christian stewardship?
- Does this have any relationship to a known evil?
- Will this draw me away from Christ in any way?

Susanna Wesley once said to her son John Wesley, the principal founder of Methodism, "Whatever weakens your reason, impairs the tenderness of your conscience, obscures your sense of God, or takes off the relish of spiritual things; in short, whatever increases the strength and authority of your body over your mind; that thing is sin to you."[3]

We must constantly guard against allowing pleasure to become a lord in our lives.

Routine Satisfaction

Most of us like familiar routines. We get up in the morning, get dressed, go to school or work, run errands, come home, eat our meals, do household chores, and go to bed every day. Because we do the same things over and over every day, our minds fall into familiar patterns. Familiar patterns help us; they guide us to do what we need to do without having to think about it. For example, we tie our shoes each morning without thinking about how we're doing it. Or if we are skilled at cooking, we toss ingredients into a bowl to bake a cake without thinking about what ingredients they are or how much of each we are using, because cooking is second nature to us. We do things every day out of habit, without thinking.

We get comfortable with our routines and in time don't even realize we have them. We just do what we do. We eventually reach a state of routine satisfaction. Now all this routine is not by itself an idolatrous state of mind, but it could lead to a problem.

We can get so hypnotized by getting up in the morning, getting dressed, going to school or work, running errands, coming home, and so on, that we become accomplished fugitives from ourselves. We do what it takes to get through the day, and we find ourselves content with doing just that.

We hear the Christian slogans that urge us to be at our best for Christ, and we know we ought to break out of our ruts. Preachers urge us to "reach for the stars," and we know that is a worthy goal. But we tell ourselves, "I'm just an average person with an average job, living in an average neighborhood. Who am I kidding? The only stars I'm going to reach for are in the cereal box in the kitchen cabinet!" So we settle for the routine we're so familiar with, and we remain content in it.

Many years ago, scientists performed an interesting experiment with a monkey and a banana. They placed a monkey in a cage and a banana outside on a shelf just in front of the cage. As expected, the monkey grabbed for the banana, but it was too large to pull between the bars of the cage.

Then the scientists took the top off of the cage. The monkey could escape the cage if it would let go of the banana and climb straight up. The monkey held tightly to the banana. Then the scientists took the back and both sides off of the cage. The monkey could escape the cage if it would let go of the banana and just walk away in any direction. Still, the monkey held tightly to the banana in spite of there being no cage!

People in a state of routine satisfaction are a lot like that monkey with its banana. It takes much less thought and effort to stay in a familiar routine than it does to break out and blaze new trails.

Routine satisfaction becomes idolatrous when our attitude toward it turns us into accomplished fugitives from ourselves. That is, we don't know who we are or what we are doing in life. We're just going through the motions and trying to make it through another day any way we can. God envisions more for our lives than that. Christians can fall into this rut as they regularly go to church, read their Bibles, and pray. They get caught in the routine of doing the tasks and lose the romance of their relationship with God.

King Saul displayed this problem, as we discussed in chapter 3. Remember the important message of 1 Sam. 15:22? "Does the LORD delight in burnt offerings and sacrifices as much as in obeying the LORD? To obey is better than sacrifice, and to heed is better than the fat of rams." God values a relationship with us more than he wants to see our pious words and deeds, especially when they are done solely in a routine.

We must constantly guard against allowing routine satisfaction to become a lord in our lives.

Self-Reliance

Parents raise children to become self-reliant. Most parents do not want a house full of dependent children hanging around in their midthirties. So if self-reliance is the goal of parenting, why does this feature make the list as a possible lord for our generation?

If we are not careful, we can grow smug and begin to feel we are responsible for our own successes in life. We begin to take full credit for all the benefits we enjoy. We begin to feel we deserve the job, the family, the promotion, and the advantages that are ours, not as a blessing from the generous hand of God, but because of our hard work, talent, and superior intelligence.

Now we might possibly think that this attitude is just a character flaw in some people and that no one would actually push it so far as to make it into a false lord. But in fact, someone did. In the middle of the nineteenth century, Ralph Waldo Emerson led an entire philosophical movement in the United States built around the ideas of self-reliance and self-sufficiency. He wrote a famous essay titled "Self-Reliance" to advance his ideas. He promoted the notion so vigorously that it became a sort of religion.

Emerson urged people to avoid conforming to tradition and society. He said we should do what we want to do and be what we want to be. This idea, along with others, formed what people referred to as a natural religion. Barely resembling Christianity, this religion was centered on the basic idea of a higher power and on humanity worshipping that higher power through communing with nature, being moral, and living simply. The main thrust of the worship of this lord was to encourage people to please themselves and look after their own interests.

Does this idea sound familiar? It should; it's one of the most popular messages of today's culture. Moreover, it's an idea as old as human nature. Jesus told a parable about a man who had a self-reliance problem: "The ground of a certain rich man yielded an abundant harvest. He thought to himself, 'What shall I do? I have no place to store my crops.' Then he said, 'This is what I'll do. I will tear down my barns and build bigger ones, and there I will store my surplus grain. And I'll say to myself, 'You have plenty of grain laid up for many years. Take life easy; eat, drink and be merry'" (Luke 12:16-19).

Listen to God's response to his self-sufficient attitude. "But God said to him, 'You fool! This very night your life will be demanded from you. Then who will get what you have prepared for yourself?'" (v. 20). This parable offers a powerful warning that we must avoid worshipping this lord at all cost! It's so natural for us to want to fall into this trap. It's so easy to depend on ourselves alone. But we need God, and we need one another. None of us is self-made, and we must never forget it.

We must constantly guard against allowing self-reliance to become a lord in our lives.

Pluralism

Almost everyone in every nation of the world experiences pluralism. People wear different types of clothes, eat different foods, practice different customs, speak different languages, and display many other differences—all of which have merged to create a new world. This new world of pluralism means that life now offers more choices than ever before. Who can say that one choice is better than the other? All options are out there, and people must decide for themselves. You do what you decide is best for you, and I'll do what I decide is best for me.

Although the pluralism just mentioned has a significant influence on people, our concern here is with another type of pluralism that is rapidly circling our globe—religious pluralism. This type of pluralism insists on equal status for all the religions of the world. It tells us we must be tolerant of all world religions and embrace them because they all contain truth. We discussed this briefly in the last chapter, referencing Peter Toon's book *Jesus Christ Is Lord*.

We want to expand on our earlier discussion by looking closer at the way our current culture urges everyone, including Christians, to conform to what supposedly is an attitude of humility and maturity when talking about religious pluralism. Admirable as this may seem, being mature and humble in this case often means being publically inclusive and accommodating of other religions, even to the detriment of one's personal beliefs. To do otherwise is to risk being labeled arrogant, immature, narrow-minded, and intolerant. Political correctness and broad-mindedness are the cultural standards that override open allegiance to personal beliefs.

Clearly, this culturally relevant attitude of religious pluralism easily becomes a lord when Christians compromise the gospel message to give other faiths equal status with Christianity. Christians, in fact, are doing this every day to keep the peace and be more inclusive in their thinking. They are blending their faith with local faiths all around them.

This blending of faiths happened a lot in biblical times. One of the best-remembered events occurred while God was communing with Moses on Mount Sinai and giving him the Ten Commandments. In the camp down below, God's people were busy blending Egyptian religious ideas with the worship of Yahweh. They formed a golden calf from their jewelry and were singing and dancing around it and throwing a big party. They were practicing religious pluralism on a grand scale.

God responded to their broad-minded religious inclusiveness swiftly and sternly: "'I have seen these people,' the LORD said to Moses, 'and they are a stiff-necked people. Now leave me alone so that my anger may burn against them and that I may destroy them. Then I will make you into a great nation'" (Exod. 32:9-10). God was ready to destroy them and start a new nation with Moses. Moses, however, interceded for his people, and God gave them another chance. The point here is that God does not wish to share lordship with any other religions or lords.

We must constantly guard against allowing religious pluralism to become a lord in our lives.

THINK ABOUT THIS

1. Think of examples of how you have been tempted to trust in human ingenuity.

2. Why can human recognition so easily get out of control in a person's life?

3. What are some good ways of controlling human recognition?

4. Why is money such a powerful lord?

5. Why will money and the things it can buy never truly satisfy those who worship it?

6. What are some best practices for not allowing the management of your personal reputation to become a lord in your life?

7. What are some best practices for controlling the desire for personal pleasure?

8. Why are people so easily charmed into making the routine satisfaction of doing their daily tasks a lord in their lives?

9. How do we avoid being charmed by the lord of self-reliance?

10. How do we avoid compromising our Christian faith in the name of broad-minded religious inclusiveness?

PRACTICE THIS

1. Fast from all technology for a period of time, that is, one day or one weekend. How hard was it to do? What did you learn from your fast?

2. Keep track each day for a week of how much time you spend on technology. Compare that to the time you spend each week with God in prayer, Bible reading, worship, and so on. Reflect on your results at the end of the week. Do you need to make any changes to your life as a result of this exercise?

3. Look at the apps on your phone or iPad. Think about the following questions:

Which ones save you time?

Which ones waste time?

Which ones improve your productivity?

Which ones are just for fun?

Which ones should you delete to be a better steward of your time and energy?

ME—PERFECT, SERIOUSLY?

CHAPTER SEVEN

Be perfect, therefore, as your

heavenly Father is perfect.

—Matt. 5:48

The first-century Jewish teachers of the Law often had ulterior motives when they asked Jesus a question. So we're never quite sure when they sought an honest answer or wanted to trick him. Nevertheless, when they asked him about the greatest commandment, Jesus powerfully answered them. His answer was so comprehensive that it basically summarized God's expectation for all humanity in our relationships with both him and one another.

Even though we're familiar with Jesus' words, they are included here for our consideration. We will be looking carefully at his answer to this question, because it gives us clear insight into how we can best make Christ Lord of our lives.

One of the teachers of the law came and heard them debating. Noticing that Jesus had given them a good answer, he asked him, "Of all the commandments, which is the most important?"

"The most important one," answered Jesus, "is this: 'Hear, O Israel: The Lord our God, the Lord is one. Love the Lord your God with all your heart and with all your soul and with all your mind and with all your strength.' The second is this: 'Love your neighbor as yourself.' There is no commandment greater than these." (Mark 12:28-31)

The Shema

These ideas Jesus expressed had a rich Hebrew heritage, dating back to ancient times. The first portion of Jesus' response came from Deut. 6:4-5 and was known as the Shema. *Shema* is the imperative of the Hebrew verb "to hear," which is how this passage begins. The passage reminded the Hebrew people that they served only one God—unlike their neighbors, who often had many lords. The passage also reminded them of their central privilege in life to love God.

The Shema named the areas of life where God's people should give attention to loving God. Hebrew rabbis down through the centuries did not analyze these aspects of a human being in great detail, so we will not do so here. However, we will look at each briefly, because each one is an area of life over which we can make Jesus Lord. As we look at each aspect, think of ways you can serve Jesus as Lord in that area of life.

Heart

The Affections

The Hebrew people thought of the heart as the location of our understanding. This is the place we find our affections, those internal desires that attract us to one thing and not another. They also attract us to this person and not that one. We must guard our affections carefully. A very small spark from deep within the human heart can quickly explode into a raging fire that gets out of control. A man nurtures an affection for a new car; a woman nurtures an affection for a diamond ring. Before they know it, they find they can't quit thinking about the objects of their affections. They are willing to do whatever it takes to own these possessions. Perhaps the worst these misplaced affections can do is cause financial problems. The next set of misplaced affections can do much worse.

A married man holds the hand of a coworker too long and affection ignites between them. A married woman gets an email from a high school boyfriend who wants to reunite after all these years. She answers the email, and affection ignites. Both scenarios create a moral dilemma and possible family crisis. So we must guard our affections carefully.

Loving God with all the heart means that he is Lord over our affections. We must honor him over the things that attract us and the people who attract us. God must be our primary love. He must organize our lives in holy ways, because he is a holy God (Lev. 19:2). In order to love him, we must love what he loves.

The Will

The heart also serves as home for our will, the resolve that causes us to stand strong for our beliefs and convictions. Even small children can have a strong will. They know what they want (candy or a toy), and they are willing to stand their ground for it. Adults do the same, for nobler causes hopefully.

Indeed, the human will in adulthood is noble when it stands for truth, justice, and righteousness. It takes willpower to make good choices in our fallen world. A stubborn, selfish will, on the other hand, can be a very ugly sight when an adult struggles for his or her own way in a business, church, or marriage. Too many relationships have shattered, businesses destroyed, and homes broken because of people with selfish wills.

Loving God with all the heart means that he is Lord over our wills: the things we believe in, the things we stand for, the things we determine for our lives. We set them all on course to honor him. God must be our primary love. He must organize our lives in holy ways, because he is a holy God (Lev. 19:2). In order to love him, we must love what he loves.

Do you love God with all of your heart as it concerns your affections and will?

What evidence supports your answer?

Soul

The Hebrew people thought of the soul as the living power within a person. It reminded them of the words of Gen. 2:7, "And the Lord God formed man of the dust of the ground, and breathed into his nostrils the breath of life; and man became a living soul" (KJV). When we reflect on this part of our being, we are reminded that we are not like the mountains, the rocks, the planets, or the stars in God's creation. They are inanimate, but they all declare God's glory in their own way. Psalm 19 begins with just such a declaration: "The heavens declare the glory of God; the skies proclaim the work of his hands. Day after day they pour forth speech; night after night they reveal knowledge" (vv. 1-2).

As wonderful as these creations are, our worship is better. Loving God with all of the soul means that God receives worship from a living, breathing person who is filled with love for him. Our affections are all directed toward him; our free will is set to honor him. That is truly special in God's sight. We are the crowning glory of God's creation, and we have the unique privilege of singing praise to our Creator.

You have made them a little lower than the angels
and crowned them with glory and honor.
You made them rulers over the works of your hands;
you put everything under their feet:
all flocks and herds,
and the animals of the wild,
the birds in the sky,
and the fish in the sea,
all that swim the paths of the seas. (Ps. 8:5-8)

God must be our primary love. He must organize our lives in holy ways, because he is a holy God (Lev. 19:2). In order to love him, we must love what he loves.

Do you love God with all of your soul?

What evidence supports your answer?

Mind

The Hebrew people thought of the mind as the place of our intellectual powers. It's that part of us that we go to school to educate. It's what teachers grade in school and mark on report cards and make a part of our "permanent record." It's the part of the brain that we continue to educate and stimulate all the days of our lives on earth. It's the blending of learning and reasoning abilities.

Loving God with all of our minds while we are in school means we give our studies our best effort. We get our homework done instead of socializing our time away. We write our term papers instead of playing video games into the night. We study for our exams instead of chatting with our friends on social networking sites.

What holds true for college students holds true for Christians in all stages of life. Loving God with all of our minds after our formal education means reading books for intellectual stimulation instead of always watching television or playing games. It means committing Scripture to memory. It means keeping our minds active with stimulating conversations about the Bible, Christian theology, and the application of Christian truth instead of settling for chats about the latest television or movie gossip, sports highlights, the weather, or the most recent Facebook updates.

Loving God with all of our minds means he directs our thoughts. God must be our primary love. He must organize our lives in holy ways, because he is a holy God (Lev. 19:2). In order to love him, we must love what he loves.

Do you love God with your entire mind?

What evidence supports your answer?

Strength

The Hebrew people thought of our strength as our physical energy. Our souls remind us that we are living beings, different from the inanimate objects of the world. Our strength reminds us that we have the physical energy to get up each morning, go out into our world, and make a difference. It calls attention to our bodies, which have to do with our physical well-being.

Here Jesus highlighted an area that is very personal to most people. Some don't even want to talk about it because they are not living the way they want to live. Their routine has them in a trap. They feel defeated but don't see a way out. This area of our lives calls attention to regular exercise, eating habits, portion sizes, types of foods eaten, the amount of food consumed daily, sleeping habits, stress management, and living a lifestyle sensitive to the health histories of our families.

In short, we must do the things that make us the best stewards of our bodies that we can be. We must consult our doctors. They can advise us on the best plan of action for all of these issues.

Along with caring for our physical bodies, we need to consider what we are doing with them. Are we using all of our energies for kingdom work and the glory of God? Do we invest our time in his service each day to bringing glory to his name? To love God with all of our strength means that God is Lord over all of our daily actions. We should have the same humble attitude of our Lord Jesus when he went about his daily activities, as highlighted in Phil. 2:6-11. Remember that most of our efforts will go unappreciated, but that's all right.

Mother Teresa of Calcutta drew our attention to the importance of doing little tasks in Jesus' name. She served people at the bottom of social structures who found themselves castaways. She ministered to those who could never repay. She labored daily with no thought of earthly recognition or praise.

Go and do likewise. Look for an opportunity today to help someone in need. Don't worry about getting your picture taken doing it. Just offer a helping hand, and in the process, you will be honoring Jesus as Lord.

God must be your primary love. He must organize your life in holy ways, because he is a holy God (Lev. 19:2). In order to love him, we must love what he loves.

Do you love God with all of your strength?

What evidence supports your answer?

Taken together these four words—"heart," "soul," "mind," and "strength"—tell us we are to love God with every part of our being. That is, we are to love God with everything conscious and everything we apprehend, everything physical and everything spiritual, everything mental and everything emotional, and everything social and everything personal. Every fiber of our being lives and breathes to love our God. We love him, not out of obligation and duty, but with a love deep within our hearts that flows from his love, grace, and mercy for us. If Jesus is Lord of our lives, then his life totally consumes our loves.

Memory Joggers

The Hebrew people knew this commandment from God, the Shema, was vitally important to their individual and community lives. So they never wanted those words to escape their consciousness. They wanted to always keep the sacred words before them. To keep from forgetting them, they didn't print them on bumper stickers or billboards, as we do today. They had memory joggers to keep the words fresh in their minds. They printed them on little pieces of paper and put them in little leather boxes called phylacteries, which they wore on their foreheads and their wrists at prayer time. God gave them this plan in Deut. 6:8. They also placed the Shema in round boxes called mezuzahs and attached them to the doors of their homes. This reminded them every time they left their homes and every time they returned of their special relationship with their God.

We have not been so physical or formal in our approach to remind ourselves to love God with all of our being. Maybe we should have been more physical or formal. Probably we would have treated this command like we treat everything else in our lives that is repetitive—that is, as a familiar routine. Then we wouldn't think about what we were doing. We would just say the words one more time.

So what is the answer to staying alert to God's command and Jesus' reminder to love him with all of the heart, soul, mind, and strength? One thing's for sure, it's not something we do by trying harder. If the command could be mastered by an act of the will, the Hebrew people would have earned an A+ thousands of years ago. They recited the Shema daily. Our love for God has to change us from within, at the depth of our being, before we can love in this complete way.

All-Consuming Devotion

John Wesley read Mark 12:28-31 and realized that Jesus was calling his disciples to an all-consuming devotion that required a superhuman kind of love. He saw a love that had to be perfected by God. In Wesley's sermon "On Perfection," preached on December 6, 1784, he made the observation that our ability to love God in this way is actually the only way in this life that we can be perfect the way God is, as Jesus called us to be in Matt. 5:48: "Be perfect, therefore, as your heavenly Father is perfect." Wesley said, "This is the sum of Christian perfection: It is all comprised in that one word, Love."[1] In his sermon "The Scripture Way of Salvation" Wesley asked, "But what is perfection?" and then answered his question with, "The word has various senses: Here it means perfect love. It is love excluding sin; love filling the heart, taking up the whole capacity of the soul. It is love 'rejoicing evermore, praying without ceasing, in every thing giving thanks.'"[2]

Wesley made practical application of this call to an all-consuming devotion to our Lord in the following prayer known simply as "Covenant Prayer." Notice how it examined the areas of life named in the Great Commandment by Jesus in Mark 12:30.

I am no longer my own, but Yours.
Put me to what You will, rank me with whom You will.
Put me to doing, put me to suffering.

Let me be employed by You or laid aside for You,
Exalted for You or brought low for You.
Let me be full, let me be empty.

Let me have all things, let me have nothing.
I freely and heartily yield all things
To Your pleasure and disposal.

And now, O glorious and blessed God,
Father, Son and Holy Spirit,
You are mine, and I am Yours. So be it.

And the covenant which I have made on earth,
Let it be ratified in heaven. Amen.[3]

God Loved Us First

The call in the Great Commandment is to love as God loves. But can we really do that by ourselves? No, not by our own will, resolve, and strength. God doesn't expect us to. God loved us first. He gives us love, and then we return love to him and pass it on to others. John reminded us, "We loved because he first loved us" (1 John 4:19).

The Old Testament Hebrew people operated at a bit of a disadvantage in keeping this Great Commandment to love God with all of their heart, soul, mind, and strength. They only had the command as a rule. Those of us who are disciples of Jesus Christ have a wonderful advantage. We have seen this love demonstrated in the life of Jesus himself. He lived it before us in ordinary daily life so we could see it on display. We considered an entire passage in chapter 4 that began with Paul's well-known words, "Have the same mindset as Christ Jesus . . ." (Phil. 2:5). Jesus gave us an example of how to love the Father.

A New Command

Jesus, no doubt, had the Great Commandment in mind on the last night he spent with his disciples before his betrayal. He gave them what he called a "new command" (John 13:34). The admonition was not new, but the motivation certainly was. The command was to "love one another" (v. 34). The motivation from the Old Testament was "as yourself" (Mark 12:31). That's probably sufficient motivation. After all, most people care for their physical, emotional, social, psychological, and spiritual needs. Since most people take care of themselves acceptably, they should look after one another just as carefully.

However, Jesus shifted the Old Testament motivation for loving others from self-regard to "as I have loved you" (John 13:34). So how did Jesus love his disciples? Think about the events of that evening. Jesus loved his disciples enough to sacrifice his life for them. He abandoned himself completely in order to save them. He placed them ahead of himself and did not claim any rights for himself. He agreed to undergo for the first time as much of a separation from his Father as he could have for his disciples and to die on the cross for them. Looking further at Paul's passage referenced above, Phil. 2:7-8 says that Jesus "made himself nothing by taking the very nature of a servant, being made in human likeness. And being found in appearance as a man, he humbled himself by becoming obedient to death—even death on a cross!"

In their closing moments together, Jesus gave his disciples a unique way the world could distinguish them as his followers: "By this everyone will know that you are my disciples, if you love one another" (John 13:35). Jesus knew responding in love the way he did was not the normal way people responded when provoked. Jesus knew treating his enemies the way he did was not the normal way the world responded. Jesus knew that his disciples did not have it within them to produce the kind of love they would need when circumstances turned against them.

Jesus gave his disciples a powerful command that night, and then he walked from that upper room and illustrated it right before their eyes. His life became an object lesson of the very love he wanted his first disciples—and us—to live in our world. Jesus went from their dinner together to the cross. The new commandment he gave was, "As I have loved you, so you must love one another" (v. 34).

Be Transformed

How, then, do we fulfill this new command of Jesus? Paul gave us a vital clue toward the end of his important letter to the Romans. Paul spent the first eleven chapters of this book talking to his readers about his theological perspective on faith in God and God's initiative in reaching out to us through Christ. Romans 1–11 was actually one long argument. Read those chapters sometime with that thought in mind.

When you reach chapter 12, Paul had concluded his long doctrinal teaching section and was ready to discuss the practical application of it. He said in verses 1-2, "Therefore, I urge you, brothers and sisters, in view of God's mercy, to offer your bodies as a living sacrifice, holy and pleasing to God—this is your true and proper worship. Do not conform to the pattern of this world, but be transformed by the renewing of your mind. Then you will be able to test and approve what God's will is—his good, pleasing and perfect will."

God has been merciful to us, not condemning us in our sins, but giving us new life in Christ. God's mercy is actually our motivation for consecration. Paul was asking, "In the light of God's mercy to us, how should we respond?" He said we should respond by offering ourselves back to him. The picture Paul painted here is that of an Old Testament priest offering a sacrifice to God on the altar. The animal's life was offered for the sin of the worshipper. The sacrifice was complete—the animal gave its life.

Our sacrifice can be just as complete. Though we're not dead, our lives can be given totally to God and his work. Jesus is our example. He offered himself for us on the cross. His sacrifice was complete because his physical life was taken. He calls us to offer ourselves to God just as he did. The big difference with us is that we go on living. But now we live with a sacrificial mind-set.

Once we have offered ourselves in consecration back to God, once we are filled with his perfect love, then we can love as he commands us to love. As we turn away from the patterns of this present age and make him Lord of our affections, will, mind, and strength, he is freed to love through us.

We notice in verse 2 that God calls us to a life of transformation. The verb of this verse is in the passive voice indicating that God is the One who is performing this miracle in us. When we consecrate ourselves to God, he works in us. We don't transform ourselves— God transforms us! God radically transforms us from what we once were to what he is making us. This transformational change begins at a moment in time with God's touch and continues for a lifetime until he takes us home.

Our lifestyle choices change, our values change, just about everything that describes us changes. We are transformed in the inner person. The inner person is the wellspring of our personality, spirituality, worship, willpower, emotions, attitudes, conscience, actions, and reactions. Everything that defines us is transformed more and more by God. Only after God transforms us can we love as the Great Commandment calls us to love.

You may wonder why we have given Rom. 12:1-2 so much coverage in a chapter on the Great Commandment. We have done this because many times Christian speakers and writers urge us to "love like Jesus loved." Well, that's easy to say but not so easy to do. We can't just will it to happen. God has to first transform our hearts from within, and then he can love people through us. In another place Paul made a similar observation, "For it is God who works in you to will and to act in order to fulfill his good purpose" (Phil. 2:13). Without God working through us, our well-intentioned efforts will be fruitless.

Conclusion

In the Sermon on the Mount, Jesus gave his listeners a great insight into his ministry when he said, "Do not think that I have come to abolish the Law or the Prophets; I have not come to abolish them but to fulfill them" (Matt. 5:17). We have seen this to be true as we have looked at his analysis of the Great Commandment. Jesus followed Hebrew tradition as he joined two parts of Hebrew law in a new way: love God and love your neighbor.

However, toward the end of his ministry, Jesus raised the motivation of that love to a completely new standard. He raised the standard high enough to call it a new commandment. This new commandment compels us to love as he has loved us! Sounds impossible, doesn't it?

The only way we can fulfill his love command is to offer ourselves to him and allow him to love through us. It calls for a completely different way of living. As his love fills our hearts exclusively, that love expels sin, selfishness, and everything else unlike Christ. As John Wesley maintained, it is the only way for Christians to be perfect—they must be completely filled with God's love. That's what

Jesus meant when he said, "Be perfect, therefore, as your heavenly Father is perfect" (v. 48).

THINK ABOUT THIS

1. What have you found to be the best way to keep your affections in line with your love for God?

2. What have you found to be the best way to keep your will in line with your love for God?

3. How do you show that you love God with all of your soul?

4. What are your greatest temptations for wasting time when it comes to loving God with your mind?

5. How do you show love for God with your mind?

6. What are your greatest temptations in controlling your physical body (weight, exercise, eating habits, stress, etc.)?

7. What are your best practices in defeating these temptations?

8. The Hebrew people had great memory joggers in their phylacteries and mezuzahs. However, the Shema still became routine to them. How do you guard against spiritual practices becoming routine in your life?

9. Why must God's love become an all-consuming devotion for us?

10. Why must we be transformed by God's grace before we can love as he intends us to love?

PRACTICE THIS

1. Write down your best practices for loving God with all of your being. Put them in order according to your priorities. Now share your list with your accountability partner or a trusted friend. Covenant together to grow in your love for God as you grow in your relationship with him.

2. Draw a large circle on a piece of paper. Divide the circle into four sections. Label each section: "Heart," "Soul," "Mind," and

"Strength." List in each section what you have committed to God of that area of your life. When you finish your four lists, pray a prayer of recommitment, reminding yourself of everything that falls under the lordship of Christ.

CHAPTER EIGHT

LORDSHIP 24-7

*Therefore, my dear friends, as you
have always obeyed—not only in my
presence, but now much more in my
absence—continue to work out your
salvation with fear and trembling,
for it is God who works in you to
will and to act in order to fulfill
his good purpose.*
—Phil. 2:12-13

Making Jesus Christ Lord of all of life runs counter to everything our secular culture teaches us. Most people in our world value, think, and live very differently than Christians do. So we can't look to our friends in the world for cues on how to live. We realize that our approach to life on just about every subject differs because we believe Jesus is Lord. When we adore him as Lord of all, we do several things:

- We give him priority over all of the daily tasks and consumer possessions that occupy most of our friends.
- We acknowledge him as Creator of everything instead of believing that all creation just happened by itself.
- We submit ourselves to him in obedience to his will for our lives instead of insisting on our own will.
- We seek to please him in all we do instead of always seeking to please ourselves.
- We think of him first and foremost in our thoughts instead of always thinking of ourselves.
- We worship and adore him as part of our daily routine instead of worshipping idols of our own making.[1]

Since our world does not offer us good examples and role models for developing a righteous life in which Jesus is Lord of everything, we must exercise extra effort on our own in completing this task. That was Paul's thought when he reminded us, "Therefore, my dear friends, as you have always obeyed—not only in my presence, but now much more in my absence—continue to work out your salvation with fear and trembling, for it is God who works in you to will and to act in order to fulfill his good purpose" (Phil. 2:12-13).

Our study takes a more personal turn as we look at daily life from a Wesleyan perspective. A Wesleyan perspective informs our thinking in several important ways. We will take into account human free will, personal responsibility, and human initiative as we discuss the topics that follow. For example, suppose a young woman wants to be used by God in a ministry assignment but doesn't know what to do. Her friend might advise her, "Just pray about it and wait. God knows all things. What God determines for your life will happen." Or her friend might say, "Don't sweat it; what will be will be."

It's true—she should pray. However, eventually the young woman will need to take personal responsibility and human initiative to let her pastor know that she is ready, willing, and able to get involved. A Wesleyan view of the sovereignty of God is not so high that we believe we should sit around and wait for him to do everything deterministically. Wesleyans believe that God works together with us in the direction our lives take.

As a word of warning about the discussion that follows, we must remember that we do not live in a spiritually neutral zone. That is, we cannot just decide to do the good, right, and true thing and consider that the end of the matter. Making a good decision is a good start, but it does not guarantee a good finish.

We must expect to receive opposition within minutes or hours of a decision to head our lives in the right direction. Often the excitement a person feels the day he or she makes Jesus Lord of his or her life is replaced the next day with the discouraging declaration, "I had no idea I would hit so many obstacles." The clouds of defeat can quickly roll in around us and bring immediate frustration to our initial resolve.

Opposition to our intentions to make Jesus Lord in specific areas of life can come from many sources. We need to be aware of these sources and how we allow them to influence us. Such sources include our non-Christian friends; the people we want to impress; the people we must interact with daily at work, school, or in the neighborhood; social media; news media; television; movies; secular music; secular society, with its expectations; Satan; and the forces of evil.

When opposition comes from one or more of these sources, we must determine that we are not going to be persuaded by their negative influences. We are going to continue with the resolve to make Jesus Lord of every area of our lives. Often the best way to win in battle is to anticipate the source of the opposition and be mentally prepared for it.

With that in mind, let's consider the following topics as a sampling of areas. For each area, we will ponder the question, "What does it mean to say 'Jesus is Lord' in this area of our lives and really mean it?"

Worldview

Everyone has a lens through which to view the world. It provides a perspective on every issue in life and shows how to fit into the world. It is made up of a person's most basic ideas of everything about life on earth. It helps a person understand, feel, and respond to everything in life. All of us actually live out our worldviews every day, usually without thinking about them.

Your worldview comes to you through your family, faith, economic situation, nationality, gender, race, history, era, politics, climate, and social conditioning. Every book you read, every television show you watch, every movie you see, and every song you hear offers you a worldview. That worldview either supports and contributes to your own or contradicts and attempts to tear away at it. Everything in culture and society interacts with your worldview daily. You seldom think about these interactions. They quietly work in your head nonetheless.

Why is the strength and viability of your worldview so important? Because the five most central components of a worldview are (1) your belief in God (or lack thereof), (2) your understanding of ultimate reality, (3) the meaning of knowledge, (4) a solid foundation for ethics, and (5) your understanding of humanity and its place on this earth.

All of these ideas are extremely important. That's why the very first area over which we need to be sure that Jesus is Lord is the worldview. A person goes a long way in doing that simply by being a Christian, reading the Bible, praying, going to church regularly, and fellowshipping with Christian friends. All of these practices inform a person's worldview.

Why talk about this? Because today in our world, many people do not believe in God. Today in our world, Christian ethics are not always commonly practiced in society. It's important to live an examined life. We must stop and think about what we believe and why we believe it. We must look for gaps or inconsistencies in our thinking and lifestyle.

Most of us go to dentists every six months, not because we think we have cavities, but because we want our teeth checked to be sure. It gives us peace of mind. It's worth the time and effort. It's also worth the time and effort to occasionally think about our worldviews.

Does your worldview testify that Jesus is Lord?

If so, how could you improve in this area?

If not, what could you do to make Jesus Lord in this area of your life?

Priorities

Tasks by the dozens call to us every day demanding our attention. We do not have the time or energy to do them all, so we decide which one is most important for the day and put it at the top of the list. Then we list the second-most important task to be done. We continue to do this until our schedule is filled—then we take a break!

Every day, emails arrive by the dozens demanding that we read them. We could not possibly read them all and do all of those tasks we just listed. So we delete the junk mail, answer our friends who want a one- or two-word reply, and print off the emails that need more research and attention. We can deal with them later.

Every day, friends text our cell phones, causing the phones to beep so that we'll reply right back. We can text a one- or two-word reply or send something longer. Sometimes it's easier to call and explain the situation in detail. It all depends on what we decide, but every beep of the cell phone demands a response.

Each morning you decide where you are going to go, who you are going to see, and what you are going to do. How do you decide all of these things? You plan your to-do list, respond to your emails and texts, and carry out your daily plans according to the priorities you set for that day.

Your priorities set the importance or rank you give to everything in your life. Much like your worldview, your priorities usually go unnoticed by you and most people until they get out of balance. When this happens, we say a man's priorities are "messed up" or a girl's are "out of line." Maybe the man just bought an expensive car instead of repairing the hole in his roof. Or maybe the girl quit high school to stay up at night and party with friends.

As you see, priorities establish a sense of purpose and direction for just about everything you do in life. If something doesn't make your priority list, it's most likely not going to happen. That's why Jesus must be Lord of your priorities. Jesus must help you decide what gets put at the top of your to-do list every day. Jesus must help you decide who gets a return call, text, and email. Jesus must work with you to set your goals and agenda for your daily activities.

Do your priorities testify that Jesus is Lord?

If so, how could you improve in this area?

If not, what could you do to make Jesus Lord in this area of your life?

Schedule

Many years ago, Disneyland featured an exhibit called the House of the Future. Scientists of that day predicted that all of the time-saving devices in this futuristic home would leave us with little more to do than push buttons and live a life of leisure.

We now live in that home of the future, but the scientists of that time were only partially correct. Although most of the devices they predicted have been invented and installed in our homes, we're busier and more stressed than ever. Now how did that happen?

Most people, including most Christians, live lives of managed chaos. They literally run from one obligation to the next all day long. As observed in chapter 6, many people have become accomplished fugitives from themselves. They are not doing anything bad; they're just trying to hold things together to get through one more day.

Many Christians say they love Jesus, but they almost never read their Bibles and seldom stop to dedicate a specific time to pray. That's like saying, "I love food but don't make time to eat it." Indeed, everyone in the world makes time for food! And everyone who truly makes Jesus Lord of his or her life makes time for Jesus.

It's all a matter of taking control of your schedule. Everybody has the same number of hours in a day. You begin with your priorities. If Jesus is at the top of your priority list, he will get your most productive time of the day for Bible reading and prayer. From there, everything else on your priority list falls into place on your schedule. At first it will be a chore to write every detail down on paper. Soon it will become second nature for you.

It's easy to say Jesus is Lord of our schedule, but it's harder to put into practice when it comes to spending time with him daily. We can get caught in the race of life without much effort, but we must decide to take control of our schedule or risk running our life away.

Does your schedule testify that Jesus is Lord?

If so, how could you improve in this area?

If not, what could you do to make Jesus Lord in this area of your life?

Relationship

Everyone comes in contact daily with friends at work, school, and in the neighborhood. These are occasional relationships. But what we want to consider here are the types of relationships where we invest our lives in one another. These are the kinds of relationships that add meaning to our lives simply by being together. We value these friendships, and they enrich our lives. Sometime we begin these relationships in early childhood and enjoy them into adulthood. And we soon learn that we do not need a large number of them. A few high-quality ones can add meaning for many years to come.

It's vitally important that we select our relationships carefully. Poorly chosen friends can lead us astray down dozens of roads away from God. A teenager who had struggled with drug abuse for several years couldn't seem to get control of his addiction no matter how many times he asked God for help. After one session of prayer at church, a counselor asked the teenager if the teenager would delete from his cell phone the numbers of his drug-using friends. The teenager refused. Several years later he left the life of drugs, but only after he had ended those bad relationships.

The types of relationships you develop will go a long way in shaping the person you become. That is why it is so important that Jesus is Lord in this area of your life. All of your friends should be people who honor Christ and who draw you closer to God. They should cause you to hunger for the things of God and companionship with the people of God.

Sometimes when teenagers want to frustrate their parents, they date people whom they know their parents would not want them to date. They delight in bringing these people home just to see their parents' reactions. Perhaps Christians sometimes subconsciously do this with God. They develop relationships with people who are not good influences, all the while knowing the Lord does not approve. Maybe, this is simply an act of childish stubborn will. We should never test God in this way. Our goal instead should be to develop close bonds only with those people who honor God and draw us closer to him.

Do your relationships testify that Jesus is Lord?

If so, how could you improve in this area?

If not, what could you do to make Jesus Lord in this area of your life?

Choices

After we set our daily priorities and schedules, we make hundreds of choices each day. Most of the time, we don't realize we're making all of those choices. As an exercise, for one day write down every choice you make. You'll be amazed at how many times you chose one thing over another.

Paul gave Timothy good advice when he wrote, "Have nothing to do with godless myths and old wives' tales; rather, train yourself to be godly. For physical training is of some value, but godliness has value for all things, holding promise for both the present life and the life to come" (1 Tim. 4:7-8). Paul was advising Timothy about making choices—deciding not to do one thing in order to do another.

Children at an early age like to make their own choices. They want to hold their own spoons to feed themselves. They want to select their clothes to wear for the day. They want to fix their hair in their own personal styles. Some of their choices seem humorous to adults, but they symbolize independence to the child.

That is why a godly influence is so important when we are young. We must all have our hearts and minds directed toward the awareness that Jesus is Lord so that we can make daily choices that honor him. As we say in our hearts that Jesus is Lord, and believe it with our minds and wills, we find ways to live out that idea daily. We start with small decisions, and then we add others until it becomes a natural, daily routine.

We never make these choices out of slavish servitude. Nothing could be further from the truth! We established that fact plainly in the last chapter. We make these choices because we love the Lord with all of the heart, soul, mind, and strength. Why? Because he first loved us and gave his Son to die for us.

Do your choices testify that Jesus is Lord?

If so, how could you improve in this area?

If not, what could you do to make Jesus Lord in this area of your life?

Attitudes

Our attitudes rest quietly behind the scenes in our lives. Yet they affect almost every area of our lives in almost every way. Attitudes are the positive or negative values, feelings, positions, or dispositions we place on people, possessions, activities, and ideas that we come in contact with daily.

We say it all the time about people. "He sure has a bad attitude." Or "She needs to adjust her attitude." We mean by this that people's attitudes are reflecting negatively on their relationships with others. We seldom stop to analyze all of the elements involved in a negative or unproductive attitude. However, as is often true, we recognize a bad attitude when we see one.

The manner in which we form our attitudes takes shape early in life. Both heredity and nurture at home contribute to shaping our attitudinal tendencies. Influences at home do not totally control our attitudes, however. That is why people with consistently sour attitudes can't blame their faulty genes or homelife; they can't say, "That's just the way I am." Because we have a free will, we make daily choices about what we allow to influence or persuade us. This is where our personal responsibility and human initiative come into play. We decide how we are going to evaluate the data coming our way about the people, possessions, activities, and ideas that cross our paths each day.

Attitudes are another area of life where we determine that we will invite Jesus to be Lord. We make the conscious decision every day to say that Jesus is Lord and display the proper attitude that witnesses to that reality.

- We choose an attitude of trust, rather than distrust, when many of life's questions remain unanswered. "Trust in the LORD with all your heart and lean not on your own understanding; in all your ways submit to him, and he will make your paths straight" (Prov. 3:5-6).

- We choose an attitude of rest, rather than unrest, when life takes a frantic pace. "He makes me lie down in green pastures, he leads me beside quiet waters" (Ps. 23:2).

- We choose an attitude of listening, rather than always talking, when others have a word from the Lord. "She [Martha] had a sister called Mary, who sat at the Lord's feet listening to what he said" (Luke 10:39).

- We choose an attitude of standing, rather than giving up, when the enemy attacks and tries to defeat us. "Therefore put on the full armor of God, so that when the day of evil comes, you may be able to stand your ground, and after you have done everything, to stand" (Eph. 6:13).
- We choose an attitude of walking, rather than giving up, when the way gets long and hard. "But if we walk in the light, as he is in the light, we have fellowship with one another, and the blood of Jesus, his Son, purifies us from all sin" (1 John 1:7).
- We choose an attitude of running ahead, rather than being led astray, when sin calls to us.

    Therefore, since we are surrounded by such a great cloud of witnesses, let us throw off everything that hinders and the sin that so easily entangles. And let us run with perseverance the race marked out for us, fixing our eyes on Jesus, the pioneer and perfecter of faith. For the joy set before him he endured the cross, scorning its shame, and sat down at the right hand of the throne of God. (Heb. 12:1-2)

- We choose an attitude of soaring, rather than remaining defeated, when the circumstances of life wear at us. "But those who hope in the LORD will renew their strength. They will soar on wings like eagles; they will run and not grow weary, they will walk and not be faint" (Isa. 40:31).[2]

Do you choose attitudes that testify that Jesus is Lord?

If so, how could you improve in this area?

If not, what could you do to make Jesus Lord in this area of your life?

Reactions

We discussed our daily actions under the heading of choices. People can tell much about who we are by those choices. They can also learn much about us by the way we react in different daily situations.

If life always remained calm, we might never react in ways that show our true inner selves. But life seldom remains calm for long.

Situations at work or at school keep us constantly on the alert. A recent television commercial illustrates this fact. A schoolboy goes down to eat breakfast and finds a table surrounded by people who brief him about his upcoming day. The first is the school bus driver, who tells him he's going to miss the bus, so he's going to have to walk to school. The second is his math teacher, who tells him she's going to give him a surprise quiz that morning. The third is a classmate, who informs him that she is going to pass him a note and get him in trouble with the teacher. The fourth is his mother, who tells him if he doesn't clean his room, he can't watch television or play video games. What is the boy's reaction to all of this bad news? He remains calm and collected. Why? He just drank his morning glass of orange juice! Wouldn't it be great if all of life's stresses were as easy as drinking a glass of juice?

Think for a minute at people's natural reactions under the stresses of daily life. Some react slowly and deliberately; others are quick and volatile. Some speak their minds; others keep their thoughts to themselves. Some use hand gestures and express themselves freely; others keep their hands to themselves. Some write letters of protest when they perceive they've been wronged; others say nothing.

We don't often think about it, but our reactions to the daily stresses and circumstances of life are another important area where we need to demonstrate that Jesus is Lord. As with attitudes, some people blame their faulty genes or homelife on their poor reactions and say, "That's just the way I am." Because we have a free will, we choose how we are going to react. Again, this is where we must exercise our personal responsibility and human initiative. We must decide to react in ways that honor Christ.

Do you display reactions that testify that Jesus is Lord?

If so, how could you improve in this area?

If not, what could you do to make Jesus Lord in this area of your life?

Moods

What mood are you in today? Are you happy, sad, angry, excited, tender, scared, or contemplative? How often do you stop to think about it? Most people rarely think about what mood they are in. They just live their lives. However, if they are in a foul mood very often, the people who live and work with them certainly notice.

Most people's moods change from day to day. Some people see more changes in their mood than others; they have greater mood swings. We all go through mood swings at different times of the month and seasons of the year. A variety of psychological, emotional, physical, and environmental factors all contribute in complex ways to this dynamic. No one can fully explain how these factors all interact to create the mood collection that belongs uniquely to each person.

The moods we are in most of the time have not been predetermined for us by fate. It may feel that way at times. We may even say, "This is how I feel right now." But when we stop and analyze each situation, we realize that we do have choices. We need to exercise those three important God-given tools of ours: free will, personal responsibility, and human initiative.

We have some control over the moods we set for our lives. This is another important area where we must learn to allow Jesus to be Lord. People sometimes say about another person, "I don't like to be around him. He drains all of the energy out of me, because he's always in such a bad mood." Or "I feel pretty good about life until after I'm around her for a while. Then I'm too discouraged to even try anymore."

Jesus came to our world to bring God's good news. That's the meaning of the word "gospel." Our Christian message is full of optimism and hope. It seems reasonable that our Christian lives should be optimistic and hopeful as well. We portray those messages not only with the words we say but also with our moods.

Do you display moods that testify that Jesus is Lord?

If so, how could you improve in this area?

If not, what could you do to make Jesus Lord in this area of your life?

Spending Habits

For most people, nothing is more personal and less open for discussion than their spending habits. We live in an age of easy credit. People receive numerous invitations every week to get new credit cards. Some of these invitations are even addressed to children!

It's easy to quit spending cash when the wallet runs dry; it's not so easy when carrying a plastic credit card. All you do is swipe the card and the purchase of your dreams is yours to take home today. That's why many consumers in developed nations are swimming in credit card debt. The average wage earner in the United States spends 105 percent of his or her annual income. How is that even possible? Credit. You just postpone the payment until next month.

Perhaps that's why so many people are so sensitive about their personal spending habits. They know they probably ought to make changes to their spending practices, but they don't want anyone else to know they have a problem. Often the issue centers on not wanting to postpone gratification. People see things at stores that appeal to them, and they want them now, so they get them.

If not guarded carefully, shopping can become a pastime that robs us of more important uses of our time and resources. There are people who have actually become addicted to shopping. They are as addicted to spending money as alcohol or drug users are addicted to their substances. They have closets full of clothes and shoes and garages full of items they don't use.

That's why when it comes to our financial resources, we need to determine that we will make Jesus Lord. Every person is as unique as his or her fingerprints, so every situation is different. That's why this matter is so personal. You must determine God's will for your life on the basis of a few basic principles:

- Look to God as the Giver of the good gifts that you enjoy financially and then thankfully respond with a 10 percent offering—or tithe—of your income back to him.
- Give offerings above and beyond the tithe.
- Organize your finances so you know how much you take in and spend each month. Spend less each month than you earn.
- Put yourself on a budget and stick to it.
- Save back a little each month to give yourself a cushion for hard times later.
- Find ways to share with other people.

In all you do in this area of personal spending habits, seek to maintain the attitude that Jesus is Lord. Come up with your plan to put God first with your finances and honor him with all you do.

Do you practice spending habits that testify that Jesus is Lord?

If so, how could you improve in this area?

If not, what could you do to make Jesus Lord in this area of your life?

Guidance

Of all of the areas of life where we seek to testify that Jesus is Lord, Christians have the most questions in the area of guidance. This section, then, will go into greater detail in exploring the topic. Divine guidance is often misunderstood. When properly understood, it offers deeply rewarding insights into our relationship with God.

If you're not like Jonah—that is, you're not holding out on God's will for your life—how do you discern what he wants you to do? Here are some methods university students have used to resolve this matter.[3]

- Some students wait for liver-shiver. You know, that strange feeling in your inner being that tells you this is not last night's pizza talking. One student, following a time of prayer, was asked if God had met his need. He responded, "No, God has not helped me yet, but when he does, I'll know. I will feel a surge of electricity flowing through my body like grasping a faulty extension cord." Such an approach is based on a preconceived notion and must be taken with caution. A person should not be overly confident with out-of-the-ordinary physical sensations.

- Some students put out a fleece, as Gideon did in the Old Testament (Judg. 6:36-40). They refer to it as putting God to the test. Although God may sometimes speak to us through signs, we should be wary of always expecting God to reveal his will through unusual manifestations.

- Some students treat the Bible like a Magic 8 Ball. Did you ever see one of those balls? They were popular years ago. People would ask the Magic 8 Ball questions. They would then shake the ball and wait for the answer to appear in the ball's window. Answers were usually vague, such as, "It's possible" or "Maybe."

  Using this method, a student asks God a question, opens the Bible to a random location, and swings his or her finger around in the air before dropping it on a verse of Scripture. Bam— God's answer is the verse. Perhaps that approach has worked for you in the past. If so, that's fine, but it's not a deeply spiritual way to discern God's will.

When Paul Little spoke at the 1973 Urbana Missionary Conference, he gave his audience the following observations about finding God's will.[4]

1. Read the Bible daily and spend time in prayer and meditation so you can become familiar with the mind of Christ through a daily relationship. Romans 8:29 says God wants us to be conformed to the likeness of his Son through this relationship. Spouses who have been married for years can usually guess each other's order at a restaurant and complete each other's thoughts in midsentence. They've spent enough time together that they know how each other is wired. Spending time in God's Word and in conversation with him brings familiarity with time. For example, you don't even need to pray about

whether you should marry a nonbeliever. God has already given his answer to that question in 2 Cor. 6:14.

2. Pray for God's will with an open mind. We must be careful not to try and save God a little time by coming to him with a request *and* an answer already worked out. Praying for God's will with an open mind is a bit risky. Praying for God's "whatever" may cause our minds to jump to some far-fetched conclusions.

   We might immediately imagine that God will send us to Bugville, No-Man's-Land, where the roaches fly and the refrigerators aren't cold enough to freeze ice. Maybe our minds jump there all too quickly because we really don't trust God fully. We're not quite sure how far God's "whatever" will take us. But as you probably already know, God doesn't work that way. He's not likely to get us in a willing position and then knock us off our feet with an off-the-charts demand. He loves us too much for that.

3. Follow the directions he gives you. As you read his Word, pray, and meditate on his thoughts, you will begin to recognize his voice, as Jesus teaches in John 10. Sheep recognize the voice of their shepherd. It's that simple. And, sheep are not the smartest animals in the livestock lot. You're much brighter, so you'll learn to recognize God's voice much more quickly. As you recognize God's voice, respond with full obedience. Making that a regular occurrence will help you grow and develop in the lordship of Christ.

   Think of children learning to walk. It's a slow, deliberate process. They take what are called baby steps, not because their feet are little, but because the steps are microscopic. That's how small your obedience may seem as you follow God's direction. However, as you continue to walk in him, as Paul describes in Rom. 8, your spiritual steps will become bigger and more confident.

4. Learn to recognize the conviction the Holy Spirit gives you. Conviction in this case does not mean the feeling of a guilty conscience. Instead, it refers to a sure resolve that God is leading you in a particular manner. This is not intended to be some sort of scientific formula that works the same for everyone. Recognizing the conviction of the Spirit is as much an art as it is a science. We're talking about conversation in a relationship with God, not uniform experiences that we all approach in the same way. Unlike emotion, the Spirit's conviction deepens with time until you increasingly sense his will for you. As Little put it, "Conviction is a deepening constant."[5] You won't always understand or get it right, but that's okay. You're not perfect, and neither are the rest of us.

5. Analyze the circumstances of your life. God often guides through these circumstances. However, do not let circumstances alone determine your decisions. They should only be one piece of a large puzzle. For example, a pastor and his wife prayed for several years about him going back to school. They sensed it was God's timing when he was accepted into a graduate school, a house opened up for them to rent, and his wife got a job all in the same week. They walked through those open doors and experienced God's help throughout the educational experience.

   However, God sometimes leads in spite of what the circumstances seem to be saying. For example, during that same pastor's first year of graduate work, his car broke down and required a major repair, bills piled up quicker than anticipated, and his wife developed allergies to nearly everything in the area. Had they looked only at their circumstances, the pastor and his wife would have packed up and moved. God's direction did not remove all the challenges.[6]

6. Seek the counsel of trusted Christian friends. The criteria for seeking a good friend who can offer you sound advice include (1) someone who lives close to God and knows his voice, (2) some-

one who is committed to following God's will, (3) someone who has experienced your situation or one similar to it, (4) someone who knows you well and will level with you. Remember Acts 15:28: "It seemed good to the Holy Spirit *and to us . . .*" (emphasis added).

7. Don't be a Lone Ranger. There is reason to be skeptical when someone makes a decision solely because "God told me so." A decision may seem bizarre, but who can question "God told me so"? That tends to stifle any open discussion. God seldom gives a person a plan of action without others sensing it. That's why a trusted friend or an accountability partner is such an advantage in discerning God's will.

8. Don't get in a hurry. God doesn't require you to discern his will quickly. You're not on a game show where you must give your final answer in thirty seconds. As you begin to move toward what you perceive to be God's will, you will sense a peaceful awareness that you are moving in the right direction. This peacefulness not only helps to confirm your understanding of God's will but also serves as a haven for your soul when difficulties arise. The pastor and his wife in the example above did not give up when circumstances turned against them during the first year of graduate school, because they had prayed until they sensed God's peace that this was his direction for their lives.

When all the factors work together in a believer's life, God has a way of confirming his will. We sometimes perceive divine guidance to be mystical and difficult to discern. That's because we tend to have distorted images of God.

We must not think of God as an ancient sage who talks in riddles that cause us to scratch our heads in bewilderment. Instead, we must think of God as a loving heavenly Father who wants to show us his will more than we want to receive it. He's more interested in the conversation than he is in our fine-tuning a master plan of action. It's in that conversation that we keep our perspective that Jesus is Lord, as we seek his guidance in all we do.

How are you doing in this area of your life?

How might you improve?

THINK ABOUT THIS

1. Why does it take so much effort to do what is good and right as Paul urged us to do in Phil. 2:12-13?

2. When we try to do what is good and right, why do we experience so much opposition that attempts to frustrate our resolve to make Jesus Lord?

3. Look back over the ten areas covered in the chapter. List three where you currently have the greatest success in making Jesus Lord of your life. Thank the Lord for his victory in you.

4. Look again over the ten areas covered in the chapter. List three where you could improve in making Jesus Lord of your life. How are you going to pursue this goal?

PRACTICE THIS

1. Look back over the questions at the end of each of the ten areas covered in the chapter and consider your answers. Develop a list of best practices that have worked in your life where you have been successful. Share your list with your accountability partner or small group this week.

2. Look again at the questions at the end of each of the ten areas covered in the chapter and think once more about your answers. This time develop a list of strategies you are going to employ in your life in the areas where you need to make improvements. Share your list with your accountability partner or small group this week.

CHAPTER NINE

LORDSHIP TRAINING 101

And we all, who with unveiled
faces contemplate the Lord's
glory, are being transformed
into his image with ever-
increasing glory, which comes
from the Lord, who is the
Spirit.
—2 Cor. 3:18

We've been on a journey together through the pages of this book. We traveled all the way back to when God started revealing himself to humanity through his name. We looked at the wonderful revelation of God's character through his different names and learned that above all, he wanted a relationship with his children.

We looked at the way God's relationships flourished and floundered in the lives of individuals throughout the Old and New Testaments of the Bible. We learned the central importance of lordship in each of those relationships. God placed those stories in the Bible, among other reasons, as examples for us to learn how to develop and maintain a daily walk with him.

We saw the way early Christians quickly recognized Jesus as Lord of both their lives and the church. Down through the past two thousand years of Christian tradition we found reminders that plainly emphasized the central theme "Jesus is Lord." Christians not only believed this truth in their hearts but also found ways to practice it in their daily lives. Often those practices ran counter to their culture. This sometimes led to opposition, persecution, difficulty, and death. They willingly paid the price when called to do so.

Now, here in the twenty-first century, we find ourselves on the stage of life. We have the stewardship of God's good news about the lordship of Christ, and, more than ever, a mandate to share God's love with our world and declare with certainty that Jesus is Lord.

Many of the things we've covered in this book are like bread crumbs scattered along a trail. We've now reached the point where we need to go back and pick up a few of those bread crumbs and refashion them into strategies for living life daily with Jesus as Lord. What follows are ten strategies to ponder and put into practice.

Strategy No. 1: Make Your First Conscious Thought of the Morning a Conversation with Jesus

Research indicates that more and more people report their first action of the morning is to reconnect with their technology. Yes, as their eyes focus on a new day, the first thing they see is the screen of their cell phone or iPad with a list of their latest emails and texts. Without realizing it, these people set a new default priority for themselves—to give their first thoughts of the day to work and social networking.

It takes a conscious effort for Christians to say, "No. I will not take my cues from society. I will give my first thoughts of my new day to Jesus." Sound countercultural? Indeed it is!

Begin your day with a prayer such as this one from the Psalms: "I call with all my heart; answer me, LORD. . . . I call out to you; save me and I will keep your statutes. I rise before dawn and cry for help; I have put my hope in your word. . . . I long for your salvation, LORD, and your law gives me delight" (119:145a, 146-147, 174). You might also begin your day with a prayer such as this one from John Wesley: "O Lord, . . . it is my duty, to love you with all my heart, and with all my strength. I know you are infinitely holy and overflowing in all perfection, and therefore it is my duty to love you. Yet not only my duty, but my joy, in Jesus' name. Amen."[1] Richard Buckner has compiled an excellent resource featuring John Wesley's prayers that you will find a helpful companion to your own prayer life. It is called *30 Days with Wesley*.[2]

Strategy No. 2: Set Aside Your Most Productive Time Each Day to Give Yourself to God's Means of Grace

We talked about taking control of our schedule in chapter 8. We observed that we should give attention to God during our most productive time of the day. If we are alert in the morning hours, we can focus our energy on our relationship with the Lord at that time. If we are more alert in the evening, then that should be the time to commune with God. The time of the day matters little. Making it a daily priority and making the most of our time with him—that matters greatly!

By means of grace, we simply intend those ordinary practices or exercises that we do regularly. God uses those practices and exercises to pour his grace through us as he transforms us more and more into the likeness of his Son. This is the thought Paul had in mind when he said, "And we all, who with unveiled faces contemplate the Lord's glory, are being transformed into his image with ever-increasing glory, which comes from the Lord, who is the Spirit" (2 Cor. 3:18).

God's transformation in our lives begins the moment we confess Jesus as Lord. He continues the transformation through a lifelong process. It comes as a divine gift but requires our honest confession of need and earnest seeking of him. We become seekers of his heart—not for an experience but for a deeper relationship with the One we love. The by-product of that relationship is greater knowledge of God and a more Christlike spirit.

God's means of grace constitutes a long list. We do not have space to consider all of them here. A partial list includes such things as regular Bible reading, daily prayer, scriptural meditation, congregational worship, the Lord's Supper, baptism, small-group Bible study, Christian fellowship, journaling, mentoring, Sabbath rest, and witnessing.[3] Make plans to study further on the means of grace and spiritual disciplines as you set aside time each day to grow in God's grace.

Strategy No. 3: Live with an Attitude of Humility before the Lord Jesus

Living daily under the lordship of Christ means always bowing our will to his will. John Wesley captured this daily attitude well in the prayer for the Covenant Renewal Service that was quoted in chapter 7. A portion of it again reads,

I am no longer my own, but Yours.
Put me to what You will, rank me with whom You will.
Put me to doing, put me to suffering.
. . . .
Let me have all things, let me have nothing.
I freely and heartily yield all things
To Your pleasure and disposal.[4]

Wesley's prayer pointed us to the words of Jesus when he reminded his disciples following Peter's great confession, "Then he said to them all: 'Whoever wants to be my disciple must deny themselves and take up their cross daily and follow me. For whoever wants to save their life will lose it, but whoever loses their life for me will save it'" (Luke 9:23-24).

The prayer reminds us to reorganize our priorities—as we reorganize our lives—according to the will and mission the Lord Jesus Christ has for us. Such a humble attitude of discipleship draws attention to our daily routine and adds substance to the familiar line we often pray from the Lord's Prayer: "Your will be done, on earth [in me] as it is in heaven" (Matt. 6:10).

Paul captured this thought well when he said, "For to me, to live is Christ and to die is gain" (Phil. 1:21). We should resolve in our hearts to go where Christ wants us to go, be what he wants us to be, do what he wants us to do. We should plan extravagantly as we factor Christ into our arrangements. In all of our decisions, the Lord attempts to save us from our own shortsightedness. Most of us tend to sell ourselves short both in our abilities and in what God might want to do in our lives. God sees our hidden potential, and he sees the almost endless possibilities as we open ourselves up to his leadership.

This kind of resolve "to go where Christ wants us to go, be what Christ wants us to be, and do what Christ wants us to do" is both a decision made in a moment and a life process. As a decision made in a moment, we decide to release control of the details of our lives and allow God to have it. As a life process, we learn day by day how to put this resolve into action. Sometimes it's trial and error; sometimes it's on-the-job training. Either way, we most often learn by doing. So we don't need to get frustrated with ourselves if we don't get it right every time.

Since being a Christian is more about a relationship with God than it is about perfect performance, you will find your best help by simply talking to him about how you feel you are doing with each area. Don't look for a perfect score in every category. Rather, look for a balanced scorecard. The trajectory of the sum total of your decisions should move you closer to full conformity to Christ and his lordship.

Strategy No. 4: Break Down the Walls in Your Life

Perhaps one of the most subtle temptations of contemporary life is the urge to divide our thinking and living into sections. We are totally familiar with the concept. For example, a large airplane has many sections: the cockpit, which is highly secure and reserved only for the pilots; the first-class cabin, which is very spacious, has exceptional service, and is for passengers of means; the business-class cabin, which has ample space and great service and is for those willing to pay more; the economy-class cabin, which features cramped quarters and entry-level service; and so on.

We expect airplanes to be divided in this way. So we may not find it strange that people tend to live their lives in separate sections as well. One activity falls into a person's spiritual life; another one falls into a person's business life. A student acts this way when he is with his school friends and that way when he is with his church friends. An individual uses these words when she is at work and those words when she is at church.

Researchers who study such matters point out that the tendency to separate our lives and minds into secular and sacred realms is one of the most distinctive shifts in American society in the twentieth century.[5] This is not a biblical way to live. Hebrew, the original language of the Old Testament, had no words distinguishing secular life from sacred life. All of life was to be lived as a single life acceptable before God—no separate sections.

That is why our analysis, in chapter 7, of the Shema from Deut. 6:4-5 and Jesus' reaffirmation to love God with all of the heart, soul, mind, and strength was a bit artificial. No ancient Hebrew rabbi would spend very much time doing what we contemporary thinkers like to do. We enjoy taking things apart and looking at each individual piece. But the Hebrew mind thinks of humans as integrated whole beings, which we are. Each of us has a heart, soul, mind, and strength. And each of us must love God completely with every part of his or her being. Nevertheless, we cannot think of one part in isolation from the other parts.

So with that in mind, break down the walls in your life that tempt you to divide it into separate sections. Tear down the partitions that allow you to act or talk one way while at work or school and a different way when at church or with Christian friends. Be the same person all the time everywhere you go, to whomever you speak and in whatever situation you find yourself. Make Jesus Lord over this one, single life you live. May people testify of you, "She acts at home the way she acts at church" or "He is the same person in private as everyone sees in public."

Strategy No. 5: Keep Your Relationship with God Up-to-Date

We have been making observations throughout this book from a Wesleyan perspective, and we will do so again here. Often when Christians mention their standing with God, they point to a moment when they prayed the sinner's prayer and asked God to forgive their sins in Christ's name. They may have the date and location they asked Jesus to become their Savior. They think back to that event the way we look back through old family photo albums to reminisce about life as it was lived decades ago.

There is nothing wrong with marking the event of becoming a Christian. There is something wrong, however, in believing that praying the sinner's prayer is all there is to becoming a disciple of Jesus Christ. Some people think they are Christians today because they prayed that prayer as a child and yet have had no purposeful interaction with God in thirty years.

A Wesleyan perspective on this matter informs us that Christianity is not one prayer prayed at a point in time but a daily relationship maintained with God. In chapter 3 we highlighted a good example of this relationship and a poor example. The exemplary relationship of Abraham showed us that he proved faithful to the call God gave him in Gen. 17:1. He walked with God daily. As a result of that daily step-by-step walk with the Lord, God found him blameless.

Saul, on the other hand, became preoccupied with the tasks and honors of being the first king of the Hebrew people. He did not take daily responsibility for his walk with the Lord. As a result he found himself dishonoring God on more than one occasion. The Lord gave him additional chances, but he never returned to the humble position from which he began as leader of the people. So in 1 Sam. 16:14 we read that "the Spirit of the LORD had departed from Saul." He went through the motions of having a spiritual life with the Lord for quite some time, none the wiser.

May King Saul be a lesson to us. It is so important to keep our relationship with God up-to-date. We maintain our relationship with God because we love him. We love him "because he first loved us" (1 John 4:19).

Strategy No. 6: Guard against the Subtle Introduction of Foreign Gods into Your Life

The time has arrived to talk about the issue that everyone recognizes but no one wants to discuss. Probably the second or third time you read about religious pluralism, you thought, *Haven't we already talked about this?* We have indeed discussed this matter more than once, but we are considering it from several different contexts on purpose.

We need to realize that we are not the first generation in history to confront religious pluralism. Some Christians wring their hands and lament that we are moving into a post-Christian society. They base their conclusion on several factors: fewer people attend their local church, fewer of their friends have respect for Christian doctrine and values, much more religious diversity exists in society, and secular culture has a more dominant voice in determining prevailing values.

It's true that many societies of our world are becoming post-Christian in orientation, but there is no need to wring our hands and lament this fact. Why? Because the religious pluralism in which we now find ourselves has been the dominant force through much of human history. It dominated most of the Old Testament world. That was the dominant religious culture in which Elijah found himself when he had his showdown with the priests of Baal and Asherah on Mount Carmel (1 Kings 18). That was the dominant religious culture in which Paul found himself when he talked with the intellectuals of the Areopagus (Mars Hill) in Athens (Acts 17). Paul walked through town and found idols honoring all sorts of gods. The people wanted to be sure they did not leave any god out, so they erected an altar with the inscription "TO AN UNKNOWN GOD" (v. 23).

While we must be sensitive to the concerns many Christians have about the religious pluralism of our day, we should keep in mind that our post-Christian culture differs little from the pre-Christian cultures of Paul or Elijah. Both of these men stood for biblical truth in their day, and so should we. They did not allow the introduction of foreign gods into their faith and neither should we.

The Lord stood by their side and remained faithful to them amid the world of foreign gods that surrounded them. The Bible is filled with examples of God's saints whom he counted faithful in the middle of overwhelming circumstances (Heb. 11). Why were they faithful? Because they had a simple, childlike faith in God. The saints listed in Heb. 11 were Old Testament individuals, so they did not have a chance to put their trust in the Lord Jesus Christ. The writer to the Hebrews follows this chapter with a passage of Scripture that exalts the Lord. With our eyes firmly fixed on him, we have no place in our hearts for foreign gods.

Therefore, since we are surrounded by such a great cloud of witnesses, let us throw off everything that hinders and the sin that so easily entangles. And let us run with perseverance the race marked out for us, fixing our eyes on Jesus, the pioneer and perfecter of faith. For the joy set before him he endured the cross, scorning its shame, and sat down at the right hand of the throne of God. (12:1-2)

Strategy No. 7: Remember That God Forgives and Restores

This sounds like such a simple truth. However, it is not as easily grasped by as many believers as you might think. We need to restate it often.

We tend to err on one of two sides. On the one hand, we falsely assume we have nothing for which we need to be forgiven, since we prayed the sinner's prayer earlier in our lives. Unfortunately, some people believe they can no longer sin after they pray that prayer. They say, "I have not sinned since the day I prayed the sinner's prayer [or got sanctified]. Everything past, present, and future is covered by Christ's blood." Paul reminded us in Eph. 2:8-9 that our salvation is by God's grace, through faith, as God's gift. We always stand in need of God's grace: "For it is by grace you have been saved, through faith—and this is not from yourselves, it is the gift of God—not by works, so that no one can boast."

On the other hand, error occurs when we fear we have failed too miserably to be forgiven by God. Some people, no matter how much others try to convince them, can never see past their failures to accept God's forgiveness. They cannot be persuaded even if someone explains that the only unpardonable sin is the unconfessed sin.

God filled the Bible with examples of individuals who received his forgiveness and restoration. We highlighted the stories of Rahab, Tamar, Bathsheba, and Paul in this book. Ruth gave us the example of an outsider whom God took into his family and made his special child. The point is, God wants to forgive everyone and restore everyone to himself. He wants a relationship with every person on this earth. No one can go too far from his love. All we must do is reach out and accept his free gift of grace, mercy, and love.

Strategy No. 8: Learn to Treasure and Ponder

One of a person's greatest advances toward Christian maturity is the ability to treasure things in the heart and ponder on them. Mary, the mother of Jesus, taught us a great life lesson in this ability. We read in Luke 2:19, "But Mary treasured up all these things and pondered them in her heart."

Some events in life are beautiful and wonderful. We treasure those memories in our hearts and ponder them for a lifetime. They bring joy as we think about them. Just recalling them puts a smile on our faces and gives a lift to our steps.

But treasuring and pondering can also be important to Christian maturity because many events in life do not make sense. People can say hurtful things. Sickness, financial reversal, job loss, family dysfunction, relationship problems, betrayal by friends, and a host of other situations and circumstances may come our way. How do we respond? How do we go on with our lives? How do you make these pieces of the puzzle fit into life's big picture?

A child putting together a jigsaw puzzle will decide a puzzle piece must go in a certain place. The child will turn it in all directions, pushing it to get it to fit. If the piece just won't go in place, the child will try pushing harder. That's exactly what we often do. We develop logical explanations for why terrible things happen. Our explanations, like the following examples, often involve God in some way:

- "Who are we to question God? God knows what is best."
- "God did this for a reason."
- "God took her for a reason."
- "His number was up."
- "Everything always happens for a reason."
- "If it is meant to be, it will be."

Most of the time, the answers don't fit at all. They are just our attempts at pushing harder to come up with a logical explanation for why something is happening to us.

Mary gave us a better example to follow. She put a set of brackets around all of the events in life she did not understand. She then put them in the back of her mind, and she went on living her life. In other words, she left life's big unanswered questions with God.

Devastating things occur in our lives that make absolutely no sense. Often we will never know why they happen. We must train ourselves to leave those matters with God—not just until we understand why they happen but even if we never understand. That is why it is important, in the good events and the bad, to learn to treasure and ponder.

Strategy No. 9: Remember, the Christian Race of Life Is a Marathon

Cars end up in junkyards for different reasons. Many were involved in accidents, but most find their way there because they just wore out. Those cars that have had the last mile driven out of them look old, rusted out, and tired from many years of service. The owners of those cars probably developed and followed a good maintenance schedule. Such a schedule helps ensure many years of faithful service for the life of a vehicle.

What is true for vehicles holds true for Christians as well. Some new vehicles occasionally go to the junkyard following a serious accident. Stephen became the first Christian martyr shortly after delivering his powerful witness for Christ before the Sanhedrin (Acts 7). Most Christians, however, will not be martyred for their faith. Most Christians will find a good role model in the example of the apostle John. He accepted Jesus as Lord and, like following a maintenance schedule, put that resolve into daily practice over the course of his life.

Throughout this book we have talked about making Jesus Lord of our priorities, our schedules, our choices, our attitudes, our reactions, our spending practices, and everything else that makes up a lifestyle. John did that one day at a time, day after day, year after year, decade after decade, until the end of the first century. Historians believe that his life continued to influence the early church until about AD 98. That's what I mean by a marathon!

Christians almost always begin their journey with Christ with an emotional rush of enthusiasm. They could run a sprint on the spot. But what about a marathon? That requires a different type of training. A marathon symbolizes a long-distance journey. The Christian life is a long-distance journey, a continuous commitment. So don't forget the example of the apostle John. Remember, the Christian race of life is a marathon.

Strategy No. 10: End Your Day by Committing Everything to God and Leaving Your Life in His Care

Your day has come to an end. How comforting to remember, God is God, and you are not. You can go to bed and leave the entire universe, along with your life and all of its cares, in his care. You can go to bed with the awareness that Jesus is Lord over all creation and its preservation. He is Lord over the nations and all humanity. He is Lord over all religion. He is Lord over the church. And he is Lord over time and eternity.

Close your evening prayer with a verse or two from the Psalms. An example might be, "O Lord, 'the sacrifice acceptable to [you] is a broken spirit; a broken and contrite heart, O God, you will not despise . . . Purge me with hyssop, and I shall be clean; wash me, and I shall be whiter than snow.' Amen" (51:17, 7, NRSV).[6]

Another option is to pray printed prayers such as this one from John Wesley: "O Lord, I want to offer an evening sacrifice, the sacrifice of a contrite spirit. Have mercy on me, O God, according to your great goodness and the multitude of your mercies. Cleanse me from all filthiness of flesh and spirit that I may follow you with a pure heart and mind. Amen."[7]

THINK ABOUT THIS

1. Why is it important for the first thoughts of your day to be about Jesus?

2. Why should your time with Jesus be your most productive time of the day?

3. Which means of grace are you finding most productive in drawing you closer to God at this point in your spiritual journey?

4. How are you tempted to divide your life? How do you guard against the temptation?

5. What are some best practices for keeping your relationship with God up-to-date?

6. Why is religious pluralism such a subtle temptation in the current culture?

7. Why is it so hard for most people to forgive themselves for their past sins?

8. Why is it important to leave things we don't understand to God?

9. Do you think it is harder to live the Christian life as a sprint or a marathon?

10. How do you best surrender everything to God at the end of your day?

PRACTICE THIS

1. Look over the list of ten strategies for living with Jesus as Lord. Select two and make them your top priorities for the next thirty days.

   a. Write out a plan of action for guaranteeing success with these priorities.

   b. List obstacles to making these priorities.

   c. Figure how you will overcome these obstacles.

d. Name an accountability partner to whom you will tell your plan of action, report your progress, and give an update at the end of the thirty days.

2. Look back over the list of ten strategies. Select another two and add to your list of priorities for the following thirty days. Again, do the following.

   a. Write out a plan of action for guaranteeing success with these priorities.

   b. List obstacles to making these priorities.

   c. Figure how you will overcome these obstacles.

   d. Name an accountability partner to whom you will tell your plan of action, report your progress, and give an update at the end of the thirty days.

3. Put the entire prayer from chapter 7 (p. 128) that is partially quoted in Strategy No. 3 on a notecard and recite it every day for a month. How does this prayer help you in your attitude about your relationship with the Lord?

CHAPTER TEN

A DAD'S PERSPECTIVE AND AN ACTION-ORIENTED RESPONSE

BRENT MOORE

Not that I have already

obtained all this, or have

already arrived at my goal,

but I press on to take hold of

that for which Christ Jesus

took hold of me.

—Phil. 3:12

As a young boy I often went camping with my family. Once we spent an entire day fishing. I lost track of how many fish I caught when my count reached thirty. I should mention that the fish were very small and were all bluegill. It really did not matter though, because I viewed myself as a skilled ten-year-old fisherman. The good memory of that day still remains with me.

While later recounting my day as a "master fisherman," it occurred to me that since I was catching and releasing the fish, I might have been catching the same fish over and over. From what I have heard, most fish (namely bluegill) are not entirely clever. They easily lose perspective and are thus prone to be caught multiple times in a short span. I suppose the same loss of perspective could be said of little boys who believe they caught over thirty *different* fish in one day.

Losing perspective is simple. Most of us get up at similar times each day of the week; we fulfill routine responsibilities; our diet, sleep, and exercise habits are mostly unchanging; and our attitude patterns are cyclical, repeating those of the previous day. These recurring behaviors—often referred to as the "daily grind"—provide continuity. Regularity prevents us from experiencing the unknown and so maintains our comfort. Most people would agree that regularity is comfortable.

Have you ever heard stories about people who win the lottery? Their worlds turn upside down, and things lose their regularity. From the outside looking in some people seem to handle the newly gained fortunes well, while others quickly lose them. You don't have to do serious investigative online reporting to find stories with the line, "Winning the lottery was the worst thing that ever happened to me." A windfall of wealth often strips individuals of all that was once considered normal.

Schedules and routines are mostly good. We observe people engaging in regular work throughout the Old Testament. The Lord also commanded his people to stop from time to time and present offerings in his name. Consider the following passage from Lev. 23:6-8:

"On the fifteenth day of that month the LORD's Festival of Unleavened Bread begins; for seven days you must eat bread made without yeast. On the first day hold a sacred assembly and do no regular work. For seven days present a food offering to the LORD. And on the seventh day hold a sacred assembly and do no regular work."

Routines can also be helpful in drawing us closer to Christ. When we are in tune with God, to his will and purpose, things are right. Being in a relationship with God requires intentionality and effort from us. It requires discipline. However, this means moving beyond just sectioning off a chunk of our day to spend with him. It means a moment-by-moment surrender of our will and agenda to God. All the while, his transcending power is at work in our lives.

Our perspectives can become skewed very quickly when this moment-by-moment surrender slips to a once-a-day encounter. Distractors from our relationship with God are everywhere. If we are not constantly on guard, we risk succumbing to evil (see Eph. 6:11-17). Sin is so brilliantly masked that it can be easily mistaken. Self-serving interests can manifest in our desires, which disrupt the perfect perspective provided by our heavenly Father. If uncontrolled, new routines emerge that oppose God's will. Our human perspective is flawed, like a fish biting at the same baited lure time and again.

The Great Shake-Up

I thought I had everything figured out as a doctoral student studying psychology. In fact, the only grade I received lower than an A was in the class Foundations of Graduate Studies. Since I had graduated with a master's degree in clinical psychology a couple years earlier, I was sure I had graduate school all figured out. So I put in very little effort toward the class and earned a B. While overconfidence is often displayed openly, it can also be subtle. For me it was faint but present and embedded in pride.

My pride also led me to put very little effort into my relationship with Jesus Christ for many years. I was not giving the Lord full control of my life. The daily grind contributed to my egocentric point of view. Life seemed safe and predictable. Since I was calling the shots, and life was running smoothly, things felt comfortable. It was not until my then eighteen-month-old daughter, Marley, was diagnosed with a cancerous brain tumor that I was jarred from my delusion.

Marley had many health-related hardships that spanned about two years before her eventual passing to heaven. I could recount many lessons learned from Marley's life that go far beyond the scope of this chapter, but I will limit them to the one point I want make. The message conveyed here is that Marley's experiences shook my life to the core. Everything that was regular and comfortable in our family's life became irregular and uncomfortable. Routine was gone!

Marley was hospitalized for about two months at Children's Mercy Hospital in Kansas City following her cancer diagnosis. She experienced a stroke, which limited her speech and control of the right side of her body. I can remember sitting in Marley's hospital room thinking about my work routine, school responsibilities, the morning and evening commute, and other mundane tasks. I realized that I was like a conditioned zombie! The moment-by-moment encounters with the Lord had been replaced with trivial earthly endeavors. Romans 12:1-2 provides these insights:

> So here's what I want you to do, God helping you: Take your everyday, ordinary life—your sleeping, eating, going-to-work, and walking-around life—and place it before God as an offering. Embracing what God does for you is the best thing you can do for him. Don't become so well-adjusted to your culture that you fit into it without even thinking. Instead, fix your attention on God. You'll be changed from the inside out. Readily recognize what he wants from you, and quickly respond to it. Unlike the culture around you, always dragging you down to its level of immaturity, God brings the best out of you, develops well-formed maturity in you. (TM)

We all encounter life's inevitable hardships. Probably all of us can recount when life's circumstances swiftly shifted other seemingly important perspectives into a different order. These events can bring us closer to the Lord's perspective. In my case, I took time off from work and school and essentially lived in the hospital for a couple of months (my wife, Nikki, spent nearly every night in the hospital until Marley came home). During all these readjustments, which included time for reflection, a veil was lifted.

I recognized that I needed the Lord and that he desperately wanted me. My time away from the daily grind was spent in prayer and devotion to him. Even though I wanted a healthy daughter and for things to be as they were before Marley was ill, my motives for pursuing Christ, as he pursued me, were pure. It was not an attempt to strike some sort of bargain. My attention was fixed on God, even as it is today. It is baffling to many people that losing a child after a two-year battle with cancer could lead me closer to the Lord.

Hardships in life can move us closer to the Lord as we listen for his direction and seek his peace and comfort. But hardships can also perpetuate self-reliance or denial. The key is to identify those instances when the lordship of Christ is not reigning over everything in our lives. Satan attempts to thwart our perspective so that we replace the Lord with other things. A clear-cut biblical account of sin interrupting God's will for his people is found in 2 Kings 17:16: The Israelites "forsook all the commands of the LORD their God." What a perfect example of hardships translating into disobedience! God simply wanted full surrender. Chapter 7 of this book made clear that the Lord wants every part of our lives (heart, soul, mind, and strength).

What follows in the sections below are some of the lessons I learned from Marley's fight against cancer and her eventual passing. Her story ties in well with the theme of Christ's lordship. Despite hardships that arose due to Marley's circumstances, our family continued to give the Lord everything. Through the process we uncovered valuable insights that have made our family stronger.

Having Faith

In teaching the theories of psychology and counseling to college and graduate students, I must back up any assertions with evidence-based research. Research is defined by Best and Kahn as "the systematic and objective analysis and recording of controlled observations that may lead to the development of generalizations, principles, or theories, resulting in prediction and possibly ultimate control of events."[1] Wow! What a mouthful! Research, and more specifically the scientific method, has improved the way humans objectively approach phenomena. However, the findings might lead to an unnatural sense of security. I rely a lot on generalizations, principles, and theories, even to the point of advocating for them. Predictions are also useful because they help us to feel empowered. We regularly make informed guesses about what to expect and consequently choose to act (or not to act) on them.

An underlying connection between routines and predictions is control. With Marley's cancer diagnosis our family was without routine, and we could not possibly predict the future. The research-oriented mind-set to which I had become accustomed had little relevance during Marley's battle with cancer. Cancer is a tricky disease for projecting outcomes. If you couple that with our living in a litigious society, you can see how our family was in the dark about Marley's prognosis.

Many people feel now what I did then. You might be reading this resonating with the notion that you have little control over your own life in some situations. Circumstances occur all the time that are not entirely under our control: job losses, abuse, infidelity, divorce, financial reversals, accidents, health problems, and so on. You might be feeling out of control. You are probably spending a lot of time and effort trying to make sense of your situation and plan what to do next. After all, that is what will offer the most comfort, right? Wrong. This demonstrates little faith in God. Self-reliance, without God's will, can be dangerous. When we put our wills before God's will, it suggests that we already have things figured out. What a prideful response to all that God has given us! Your hardship is an incredible opportunity for a change of perspective. Seek out the Lord in prayer, Scripture, and accountability for a fresh perspective.

Actively Participating

In chapter 8, our personal responsibility in making and maintaining Christ as Lord over everything was emphasized. When we adopt a Christ-centered perspective, we must participate accordingly. We are not observers on the sidelines. When we pray for something, we should be doing our part to bring the petition to fruition when possible.

My academic training is geared toward understanding people and helping them. In fact, by profession, as an educator in the field of counseling at a university, I train people to help others. It is painful for me to see others who want and expect to receive help but resist working toward that help. It is a paradox in action, and counselors must work around this obstacle. If clients who desire counseling unrealistically expect results without working through the therapy I recommend, what then do some people expect from an omnipotent heavenly Father without doing their own work?

When Marley was ill with cancer, Nikki and I prayed to God incessantly for her healing. We also did everything we knew possible to physically, mentally, and emotionally help her cope with the circumstances on this side of eternity. We were active participants in attempting to make her well.

It does not undermine the lordship of Christ to pray for something and then work toward the request through our human efforts. We are expected to work toward the outcome. If God has called someone to become a doctor, but that person decides not to study and only prays to God that all of his or her exams go smoothly, what is the likelihood that the person will pass medical school? We must do our part to accomplish God's will. This seems like a given, but it applies to so many situations that people encounter daily.

Think about the most pressing issues you are currently facing. Do you actively pray about them? Do you actively work toward improving or resolving them? These two questions are not mutually exclusive. Our efforts to work toward solutions are often flawed by our human perspective. We should be praying about how to effectively deal with the problems confronting us. Again, this requires surrendering our natural responses to God's guidance.

God already knows what we need and what we want. It is still necessary to seek the Lord in prayer. In *The Magician's Nephew* by C. S. Lewis, three characters were on a mission that Aslan (a lion representing Christ) had given them. Polly and Digory were without food, but their talking horse, Fledge, had plenty of good grass to eat. Their discourse went as follows:

"Well, I *do* think someone might have arranged about our meals," said Digory.

"I'm sure Aslan would have, if you'd asked him," said Fledge.

"Wouldn't he know without being asked?" said Polly.

"I've no doubt he would," said the Horse (still with his mouth full [with grass]). "But I've a sort of idea he likes to be asked."[2]

Relying on human intuition is a natural response. When faced with a problem, using solutions that have succeeded in the past is common. So if we face a new circumstance, we might use old solutions. The old solutions might not work. In psychology this is called functional fixedness. We have the resources to work out the problem but are blind to the solution because of our fixed ways. Some people wear themselves out without accomplishing anything; they think they are working toward a solution, but they are really spinning their wheels. Ask Christ to give you direction as you work toward your petitions made to him.

The Bible also offers valuable perspectives about how to improve or resolve problems. Nevertheless, there is a lot of literature designed and marketed for self-help. The academic community attempts to make sure that literature is legitimate before consuming it. In my field of study, students are urged to seek out peer-reviewed journal articles that empirically validate the best options for a given problem. "Go to the databases," college instructors say. When the scientific studies are lacking, another option is to rely on philosophy. Thomas Kuhn wrote, "As I have shown elsewhere, the analytical thought experimentation that bulks so large in the writings of Galileo, Einstein, Bohr, and others is perfectly calculated to expose the old paradigm to existing knowledge in ways that isolate the root of crisis with a clarity unattainable in the laboratory."[3] With so many shifting paradigms throughout history, it is incredible that the Bible continues to illuminate everything. The Bible trumps them all! From science to philosophy, the Bible reveals wisdom about handling our concerns.

Death Avoidance

For Nikki and me the grief of losing our child was tremendous. C. S. Lewis wrote about loss in *The Lion, the Witch, and the Wardrobe* when Susan and Lucy were grieving for Aslan after the Witch tortured and killed him.

> I hope no one who reads this book has been quite as miserable as Susan and Lucy were that night; but if you have been—if you've been up all night and cried till you have no more tears left in you—you will know that there comes in the end a sort of quietness. You feel as if nothing is ever going to happen again. At any rate that was how it felt to these two.[4]

Death is traumatic for most human beings. The topic of death is sidestepped by many because it is uncomfortable to think about, let alone discuss. Immortality, on the other hand, is revered for good reason—but often in strange places. I am shocked at the popularity and prevalence of science-fiction movies that depict immortality. Superhero movies top the box-office charts around the world. Some of the popularity might have to do with the action sequences, the computer-generated effects, an affinity for the associated comic book, or a story line. Probably some of the draw to superhero films is the invincibility of the main character. Many superheroes have a weakness, but for the most part, they rarely die.

The clearest revelation I had following Marley's death is that everyone will die someday. This is another obvious life lesson. However, most of us do not think about death often because we remain too busy. I spent many of my days going through the daily grind, the routine I mentioned earlier. When I did have an opportunity (or rather made the opportunity) to think and reflect, matters of little eternal value consumed me. However, when I saw someone whom I loved and for whom I cared transition from earth to heaven, the most important things in life became outrageously apparent.

I was teaching six college classes when Marley passed away. Following her funeral, I took several days to collect myself before returning to work. I can remember the course topic very well for four of the classes I was teaching on my return. It was "learning." I looked at my classes movingly and, addressing approximately 160 students, stated that the principles of learning did not matter! However, the students had to know the material because the psychology department mandated it, so I reluctantly shared the information on the tentative course schedule. But all along, my mind was reflecting on more existential matters. The Lord's will and purpose for my life was at the forefront of my mind. I also recognized that my existence on this earth is limited. My time on this earth is constantly drawing nearer to the end, and I should make every moment count. First Corinthians 7:29-31 states,

> What I mean, brothers and sisters, is that the time is short. From now on those who have wives should live as if they do not; those who mourn, as if they did not; those who are happy, as if they were not; those who buy something, as if it were not theirs to keep; those who use the things of the world, as if not engrossed in them. For this world in its present form is passing away.

There will be a moment in your life when you breathe a final breath and your physical body will remain on earth. Don't avoid thinking about death! My mind drifts on occasion to Marley's lifeless body on our living-room sofa. Everyone had left the house so my wife and I could spend a final moment with her body. It was not the same. Don't get me wrong; I cherished every last moment I could lay my eyes on her, because my memories with her rushed through my head. But Marley's personhood no longer resided in her body. Her soul had gone to heaven. The part that we loved most about Marley was absent to us.

Take a moment to reflect on your life right now. Are you serving Christ as Lord? Do you revere his name as Lord over all? You are in a unique position because there is time to discern God's will and follow him. I don't know about you, but if I end up living a long life, I want to be able to look back knowing that I was operating in God's will at the end of it all. There will be no regrets. My worldview has changed because I look at Marley's passing as a point of reference. I can look at my baby pictures and know where I began. I go to Marley's gravesite and know where my body will end—lying next to hers. This is precious time that God has granted me. So the same can be said of you. What will you do with it?

Final Thoughts

You have read about what the lordship of Christ means from a historical perspective. You can even describe what the lordship of Christ means personally to you as a believer. But what are you going to do differently about it? There is always room for improvement as we journey with Christ. Perhaps this could be a catalyst for Christ to do something new in you.

Ending a book about the lordship of Christ using lessons learned through the loss of my daughter is both fitting and daunting. I would like my chapter to conclude by emphasizing that no matter the circumstance—big or small, horrific or benign, conspicuous or hidden—God remains Lord over all. I will testify to God's faithfulness even amid something that is a tragedy from my human perspective.

THINK ABOUT THIS

1. Identify the routine parts of your day. What are the advantages to routine? What are the disadvantages?

2. List the distractors present in your culture that could potentially impact your spiritual walk? Which ones are obvious? Which ones are subtle?

3. Think about how you construct reality around previous experiences and generalizations. How do biblical principles inform these perspectives?

4. When do you feel closest to God? How does your perception of control over situations influence your relationship with God?

5. What do you believe God wants from you right now? What changes need to be made in order to accommodate God's desires for you?

6. Rank in order the things you deem important. Does this list reflect God's mandates for you?

7. Realistically, what can you do to make every moment of your existence worthwhile?

PRACTICE THIS

1. Develop a Christ-centered statement to help refocus your attention on God. Practice repeating this statement to aid in making a moment-by-moment surrender to God.

2. Closely monitor your feelings for one day. Recognize the times when you feel deep pleasure or satisfaction. Determine the source of these feelings. Now give God the glory!

3. Pray for ways that you can work alongside God to help fulfill your prayer requests. Make a list of ways to accomplish this end. Think creatively and have fun! For example, after praying

for the healing of someone who is sick, write a letter of encouragement and drop it in a card to that person. Involve other people and be imaginative about ways to boost morale amid the circumstances.

4. Find someone who is going through a hardship. Do an act of kindness for that person. Consider also doing an act of kindness for a caretaker. Do not ask what you can do for the person! Think of something and just do it. Try also making the act anonymous.

5. Make a list of ways that God has been faithful to you. Keep it in a prominent place to remind you of his faithfulness.

N●TES

Chapter 1

1. For twenty years Sue and I took university students on mission trips to underdeveloped countries.

2. I know my grandparents lived that way. They grew their own food and stayed on the farm for weeks at a time, content with their self-contained existence.

3. I have flown to some of the most remote areas of the world. When I get off the plane, I am usually greeted with the sight of satellite dishes and cell phones! I have found strong cell phone signals to call my wife, Sue, in the jungles of central Africa and South America, as well as on islands in the middle of the Pacific Ocean. I'm amazed every time at how interconnected our world is.

Chapter 2

1. Lane Zachary, comp., "He Is Lord," in *He Is Lord! More "Reasons to Sing"* (Kansas City: Lillenas Publishing, 1971), 1. My personal confession that Jesus is Lord is tied to this chorus. Decades ago, at an old Christian campground in the mountains, teens from churches across the northern half of my state had gathered for a week of recreation, outdoor sports, Bible study, and church services. At the Monday evening worship service, the song leader presented to us the new arrangement of the chorus. We sang it several times during that service to get it in our minds, and then we sang it mornings and evenings throughout the week to memorize it thoroughly.

2. Werner R. Kramer, *Christ, Lord, Son of God*, trans. Brian Hardy (Naperville, IL: Alec R. Allenson, 1966), 20-21.

3. See Acts 3:15; 4:10; 10:40; 13:30; Rom. 7:4; 8:11; 1 Cor. 15:3-5, 12-20; Eph. 1:20; Col. 2:12; 1 Thess. 1:10; 2 Tim. 2:8; and 1 Pet. 1:21.

4. Kramer, *Christ, Lord, Son of God*, 65.

5. Ibid.

6. Ibid., 19-20.

7. Ibid., 67.

8. Ibid., 72.

9. Ibid., 67.

10. *Book of Common Prayer* (New York: Church Hymnal Corporation, 1979), 120.

11. Ibid., 358-59.

12. Ibid., 864-65.

13. Zachary, "He Is Lord," 1.

Chapter 3

1. Kenneth Barker, ed., *Reflecting God Study Bible* (Grand Rapids: Zondervan Publishing House, 2000), 30.

2. Ibid., 274.

3. M. G. Easton, "Lord," in *Easton's Bible Dictionary* (Oak Harbor, WA: Logos Research Systems, 1996), Logos Bible Software.

4. Barker, *Reflecting God Study Bible*, 274.

5. Examples of this occur in Gen. 20:4; Exod. 4:10, 13; 15:17.

6. Easton, "Lord," in *Easton's Bible Dictionary*.

7. Barker, *Reflecting God Study Bible*, 90.

8. Ibid., 93.

9. Ibid.

10. Depending on the English version, *Adonai* is also translated using the word "lord," but only the first letter is capitalized. The name Adonai is sometimes used in combination with other names for God. In many English versions, the name Lord GOD translates the Hebrew *Adonai Yahweh,* and the name LORD God translates *Yahweh Elohim.* The NIV translates the Hebrew "Sovereign LORD" and "LORD God," respectively.

11. Claus Westermann, *Genesis 12–36: A Commentary,* trans. John J. Scullion (Minneapolis: Augsburg Publishing House, 1985), 259.

12. I wrote this sentence carefully. According to my understanding of Scripture, I do not believe Abraham willfully disobeyed a known law of God according to his level of understanding.

13. See Judg. 2:11; 10:10; 1 Kings 18:18; Jer. 2:23; Hos. 2:17.

14. Easton, "Baal," in *Easton's Bible Dictionary*.

15. Ibid.

16. See Exod. 34:13; Judg. 6:25; 1 Kings 16:33; 2 Kings 23:6, KJV.

17. If you'd like to read more on Baal worship in the twenty-first century, see Al Truesdale, *The Baal Conspiracy* (Kansas City: Beacon Hill Press of Kansas City, 2010). You'll be amazed at how contemporary the subject is.

18. Bruce B. Barton et al., *Galatians,* Life Application Bible Commentary (Carol Stream, IL: Tyndale House, 1994), 120.

Chapter 4

1. Easton, "Jehovah," in *Easton's Bible Dictionary*.

2. Peter Toon, *Jesus Christ Is Lord* (Valley Forge, PA: Judson Press, 1978), 32.

3. Ibid., 33.

4. Ibid., 34.

5. Kramer, *Christ, Lord, Son of God,* 68.

6. Toon, *Jesus Christ Is* Lord, 35.

7. Ernest Lussier, *Jesus Christ Is Lord: Adoration Viewed through the New Testament* (New York: Alba House, 1979), 21-22.

8. Ibid., 23.

9. Remember that Luke wrote about this miracle after Jesus' resurrection. Thus the early church recognized Jesus' divinity by the time of Luke's writing. It's as if Luke was indicating to his readers that events such as the raising of the widow's son from the dead were clear signs of Jesus' divinity even during his ministry.

10. Lussier, *Jesus Christ Is Lord*, 31.

11. Kramer, *Christ, Lord, Son of God*, 68-69.

12. Toon, *Jesus Christ Is Lord*, 40-41.

13. Kramer, *Christ, Lord, Son of God*, 78.

14. Ibid., 79-80.

Chapter 5

1. Manya Bracher, "Atheists Roll Out Ad Campaign," The Seeker, *Chicago Tribune*, May 22, 2009, http://newsblogs.chicagotribune.com/religion_theseeker /2009/05/atheist-bus-campaign.html.

2. This statement was made during a debate I had with an atheist on a radio talk show in the fall of 2012. We got along just fine personally, though our religious beliefs were miles apart.

3. See also 2 Cor. 4:4 and Heb. 1:3, which indicate that Christ perfectly represents the triune God to us.

4. Lussier, *Jesus Christ Is Lord*, 29.

5. We must not conclude from this passage that when Christ turns all creation over to his Father that he is substantially inferior to him. This passage does not imply subordinationism, as some suggest. All three persons of the Trinity are equal in deity; they have the same substance or essence. The apparent subordination in this passage is one of function. The Son carries out the Father's will. In the end, the triune God will be recognized by all creatures as supreme and sovereign over all reality.

6. Toon, *Jesus Christ Is Lord*, 101-13.

7. Ibid., 113-19.

8. Much more could be said on comparative religions, but space does not permit it. If you have an interest in this subject from an evangelical perspective, see the following two books by Winfried Corduan: *Neighboring Faiths: A Christian Introduction to World Religions* (Downers Grove, IL: InterVarsity Press, 1998) and *A Tapestry of Faiths: The Common Threads between Christianity and World Religions* (Downers Grove, IL: InterVarsity Press, 2002).

9. Bruce B. Barton et al., *1 Peter, 2 Peter, and Jude*, Life Application Bible Commentary (Carol Stream, IL: Tyndale House, 1995), 107-8.

10. Toon, *Jesus Christ Is Lord*, 42.

Chapter 6

1. Toby McKeehan and Mark Heimermann, "Jesus Freak," in *Contemporary Christian: Guitar Chord Songbook* (Milwaukee: Hal Leonard Corporation, 2004), 114-17.

2. Internet Movie Database, s.v. *"Life with Judy Garland: Me and My Shadows* (2001)," http://www.imdb.com/title/tt0250581/trivia?tab=qt (accessed April 22, 2013).

3. Henry Moore, *The Life of the Rev. John Wesley, A.M.* (London: John Kershaw, 1824), 1:125.

Chapter 7

1. John Wesley, "On Perfection," in *The Works of John Wesley*, 3rd ed. (Grand Rapids: Baker Book House, 1979), 6:413.

2. Wesley, "The Scripture Way of Salvation," in *Works of John Wesley*, 6:46.

3. John Bowling, *Above All Else: 20 Years of Baccalaureate Sermons* (Kansas City: Beacon Hill Press of Kansas City, 2012), 234-35. Adapted from John Wesley, "Wesley Covenant Prayer," PediaView.com, http://pediaview.com/openpedia /Wesley_Covenant_Prayer.

Chapter 8

1. Adapted from Lussier, *Jesus Christ Is Lord*, ix.

2. Adapted from Frank Charles Thompson, ed., "Seven Attitudes of the Spiritual Life," in *The Thompson Chain-Reference Bible*, 2nd ed. (Indianapolis: B. B. Kirkbride Bible, 1990), list no. 3242.

3. These are just a few examples of what I've heard from students during the twenty-eight or more years I've worked with them. In that time, I think I've heard just about every method for finding the will of God.

4. David M. Howard, ed., *Jesus Christ: Lord of the Universe, Hope of the World* (Downers Grove IL: InterVarsity Press, 1974), 76-80.

5. Ibid., 78.

6. These examples are the experiences Sue and I had surrounding my attendance at Vanderbilt University in Nashville.

Chapter 9

1. Merritt J. Nielson, ed., *Ashes to Fire Year B Devotional: Daily Reflections from Ash Wednesday to Pentecost* (Kansas City: Beacon Hill Press of Kansas City, 2011), 79.

2. Richard Buckner, ed., *30 Days with Wesley* (Kansas City: Beacon Hill Press of Kansas City, 2012).

3. For further study, I have written a book on spiritual disciplines titled *Rendezvous: A Sacred Encounter with God* (Kansas City: Beacon Hill Press of Kansas City, 2007).

4. Bowling, *Above All Else*, 234-35.

5. Robert N. Bellah et al., *Habits of the Heart: Individualism and Commitment in American Life* (Berkeley, CA: University of California Press, 1985), 43.

6. Nielson, *Ashes to Fire Year B Devotional*, 44.

7. Ibid., 31.

Chapter 10

1. J. W. Best and J. V. Kahn, *Research in Education*, 10th ed. (Boston: Pearson, 2006), 25.

2. C. S. Lewis, *The Magician's Nephew*, in *The Chronicles of Narnia* (New York: HarperCollins, 1982), 87.

3. T. S. Kuhn, *The Structure of Scientific Revolutions*, 2nd ed. International Encyclopedia of Unified Science, vol. 2, no. 2 (Chicago: University of Chicago Press, 1970), 88. The author is referencing his work "A Function for Thought Experiments," in *Mélanges Alexandre Koyré*, ed. R. Taton and I. B. Cohen (Paris: Hermann, 1963).

4. Lewis, *The Lion, the Witch, and the Wardrobe*, in *The Chronicles of Narnia*, 183.

BIBLIOGRAPHY

Barker, Kenneth, ed. *Reflecting God Study Bible*. Grand Rapids: Zondervan Publishing House, 2000.

Barton, Bruce B., Mark Fackler, Linda K. Taylor, and Dave Veerman. *1 Peter, 2 Peter, and Jude*. Life Application Bible Commentary. Carol Stream, IL: Tyndale House, 1995.

Barton, Bruce B., Linda K. Taylor, David R. Veerman, and Neil Wilson. *Galatians*. Life Application Bible Commentary. Carol Stream, IL: Tyndale House, 1994.

Bellah, Robert N., Richard Madsen, William M. Sullivan, Ann Swidler, and Stephen M. Tipton. *Habits of the Heart: Individualism and Commitment in American Life*. Berkeley, CA: University of California Press, 1985.

Best, J. W., and J. V. Kahn. *Research in Education*. 10th ed. Boston: Pearson, 2006.

Easton, M. G. *Easton's Bible Dictionary*. Oak Harbor, WA: Logos Research Systems, 1996. Logos Bible Software.

Howard, David M., ed. *Jesus Christ: Lord of the Universe, Hope of the World*. Downers Grove, IL: InterVarsity Press, 1974.

Kramer, Werner R. *Christ, Lord, Son of God*. Translated by Brian Hardy. Studies in Biblical Theology 50. Naperville, IL: Alec R. Allenson, 1966.

Kuhn, T. S. *The Structure of Scientific Revolutions*. 2nd ed. International Encyclopedia of Unified Science, vol. 2, no. 2. Chicago: University of Chicago Press, 1970.

Lewis, C. S. *The Chronicles of Narnia*. New York: HarperCollins, 1982.

Lussier, Ernest. *Jesus Christ Is Lord: Adoration Viewed through the New Testament*. New York: Alba House, 1979.

Nielson, Merritt J., ed. *Ashes to Fire Year B Devotional: Daily Reflections from Ash Wednesday to Pentecost*. Kansas City: Beacon Hill Press of Kansas City, 2011.

Thompson, Frank Charles, ed. *The Thompson Chain-Reference Bible*. 2nd ed. Indianapolis: B. B. Kirkbride Bible, 1990.

Toon, Peter. *Jesus Christ Is Lord.* Valley Forge, PA: Judson Press, 1978.

Wesley, John. "On Perfection." In vol. 6, *The Works of John Wesley*, 411-24. 3rd ed. London: Wesleyan Methodist Book Room, 1872. Reprint, Grand Rapids: Baker Books, 1979.

———. "The Scripture Way of Salvation." In vol. 6, *Works of John Wesley*, 43-54.

Westermann, Claus. *Genesis 12–36: A Commentary.* Translated by John J. Scullion. Minneapolis: Augsburg Publishing House, 1985.

Zachary, Lane, comp. "He Is Lord." In *He Is Lord! More "Reasons to Sing,"* 1. Kansas City: Lillenas Publishing, 1971.